"One of the most interesting and innovative approaches to business success. A must-have for any business library."

—Dr. Andrew Raleigh

Laberinto

Laberinto

A Tool from the Past for Business Success Today

Deborah Gonzalez, Esq.
Executive Vice-President, Parker Associates International

iUniverse, Inc.
New York Lincoln Shanghai

Laberinto
A Tool from the Past for Business Success Today

iUniverse books may be ordered through booksellers or by contacting:

iUniverse
2021 Pine Lake Road, Suite 100
Lincoln, NE 68512
www.iuniverse.com
1-800-Authors (1-800-288-4677)

ISBN-13: 978-0-595-40730-9 (pbk)
ISBN-13: 978-0-595-85095-2 (ebk)
ISBN-10: 0-595-40730-7 (pbk)
ISBN-10: 0-595-85095-2 (ebk)

Printed in the United States of America

Dedication

To: Ruth

Contents

Acknowledgments

Thank you to:

Ana, Adelfo, Alex, Andrew, Angelica,
Diego, Gabriel, Hector, Ivette, Jackie, JM, JR, Julio,
Marta, Mary, Naomi, Penny, Rafael, Richard,
Roberto, Rosa, Vickie, Vivian, Xiomara, Yvonne,
And you, the reader.

Introduction

Going back in time, back in history, to learn the important lessons of how to achieve success today is not new. This is what the Renaissance was about—the rediscovery of ancient man's wisdom through the teachings of Aristotle, Plato and Socrates. The belief was that the ancient Romans and Greeks knew things that the Medieval Europeans had forgotten—that was why the world was in turmoil—we must return to a past time—a glorious time and bring that glory back to the present. Leonardo da Vinci did it, and so did many others, including the business tycoons of that earlier time—the Medici's—and the lead corporation of the time—the Catholic Church. Is it so surprising then that in today's business literature so many authors have looked back to the 15th century—to Leonardo himself—to find the secrets of success for today? Titles such as: "How to Think like Leonardo da Vinci;" "If Socrates Ran General Motors;" "What Would Machiavelli Do?" "Power Plays: Shakespeare's Lessons in Leadership and Management;" "Elizabeth I as CEO;" are just the tip of the iceberg. Then there are those books that include a religious basis: "The Five Rings for Business;" "The Art of War for Business;" "Jesus as Your CEO", even "The Tao of Pooh."

As the very, very brief list above provides, business professionals are fortunate in this free market economy to be able to choose from a vast selection of historical figures as business gurus and role models including: Plato, Brunelleschi, Columbus, Copernicus, Elizabeth I, Shakespeare, Thomas Jefferson, Benjamin Franklin, Charles Darwin, Gandhi, Einstein, etc., etc., etc. But since we are talking business, and business books are fierce competition, and in this genre, the success of a business book is who can go back the farthest, I will attempt to beat them all! I will not go back to the 15th century (regards to Master da Vinci) or to the 1st century (too dirty and inconvenient for my taste) but to the beginning of man's awareness of inner reflection—prehistory (which is "the time before man had writing to give us history")—in fact, I will take you to a time before words, when symbols was the only language humans needed to understand each other.

We are going back, back, back to the—

Laberinto.

Nice word, heh? What does it mean? *Laberinto* is Spanish for *Labyrinth.* So why did I not call my book "Labyrinth: A Tool for Business Success?" Would you have bought it with that title? *Labyrinth* is so new-agy—so out there—so spiritual—and you are a nuts and bolts down to business person searching for a quick silver bullet to become more successful. *Labertinto* sounds a little more technical, more business like, more professional. Or maybe not? I like it better in Spanish anyway, and in today's global society we can use a few more foreign words introduced into the business lexicon, don't you think? Business is inter-national, and English can't have the monopoly on buzz words—but that's another discussion.

I am taking you back to the time of the laberinto—a symbol that is disputed as to its definition and the imitators who try to supplant it in our minds—mazes, spirals, nautilus, confusing passageways—none of these are what we seek for our work today. So now that you are even more confused and confusion is bad for business let me set you straight.

A *laberinto* is a self-contained unicursal continuous path leading to a center that leads back out again on the same path. It is usually circular in form but is not required to be so to be defined as a *laberinto*. It must however, adhere to certain basic conditions:

1. it must have an entry point that will serve as an entrance and an exit;

2. it must go in only one direction with no choices to be made and no obstacles to be overcome;

3. it repeatedly folds in on itself, leading you past the center a number of times;

4. it must have a center; and

5. the only way out is the path that led you in.

Figure 1 Cretan 7-circuit Classical Labyrinth

As I was trying to explain to my business partner why I was writing a book about the *laberinto* as a tool for business success he stated manner-of-factly "Why not? We are all walking around in circles anyway."

You can see that the actual word *labyrinth* has been misused and misapplied in everyday language—in fact this misuse is condoned by the authorities:

The American Heritage Dictionary of the English language defines a *labyrinth* as: 1. An intricate structure of interconnecting passages through which it is difficult to find one's way; a maze. 2. Something highly convoluted in character, composition or structure.

But perhaps, "misuse" is too strong a word. *Labyrinth* has been "redefined" to make it more relevant in our common language. And here is the **first lesson** of the *laberinto* for business—**if you do not watch how you define yourself, others will redefine you in their own interest**—and it may be very different from what you feel your business truly is.

Laberintos or at least labyrinthine forms have been found on every continent except Antarctica—the list of countries is impressive: Germany, Egypt, Finland, India, Estonia, Jericho, Nepal, Denmark, Ecuador, England, Russia, Brazil, South Africa, China, Ireland, Italy, Syria, Iraq, Australia, Spain, The United States, and Peru. The largest concentration of pre-modern *laberintos* are in Scandanavia. But modern ones outnumber the ancient paths left by our ancestors. Today there are over 1000 *laberintos* in the United States alone[1]. Truly an international trademark—a symbol understood on its own.

Laberintos have been made from tiles, sea shells, turf, and paint and have been found on stone carvings, cave paintings, clay tablets, mosaic floor tiles, tree bark, Neolithic rock art, petroglyphs, pottery decorations, coins, graffitos, jewelry, floor pavements, stain glass, renaissance portraits and manuscripts. They have been located by the sea and between mountains; in medieval cathedrals and Pakistani mosques.

They have been used for protection in childbirth (India), to teach lessons, to offer hope of the afterlife, for prayer, to trap demons and evil spirits (Scandanavia), and even as Chinese temple clocks (*hsiang lu*) by being the form the powdered incense is burned in. They have been used as games (North African Zulu's *usogexe*), as dance steps (Ancient Greek Crain Dancing) and as "dreaming tracks" of the Australian aborigines. It is even argued that they served in some form of astrological function or as calendars or maps. But how, we do not know. We do know they were used as substitutes for great cities—a pilgrimage to Jerusalem or as a reenactment of the great battle for Troy.

This most archetypal of symbols can be found all around us: from the folds of coral and the internal structure of the Nautilus shell to the queue settings of Disneyland rides[2]; in the monastic library of Melk in the novel and film *In the Name of the Rose* and Dorothy's yellow-brick road from *The Wizard of Oz*, to

---

1. Why so numerous? There are different theories as to why labyrinths enjoy resurgence at certain times in history and why they are so common today. "The adaptability of the basic labyrinth design, contrasting with the complexity of its symbolism, appeals to both the spiritual and secular aesthetic of artist, patron and public alike, whatever its setting." Jeff Saward, Labyrinths and Mazes, pg. 136
2. "Disneyland provided similar structured excursions within its fantasy rides—the ride itself is the experience, but to handle the crowds, query is inevitable. This problem is turned into an opportunity, with lines of visitors constantly on the move, passing through one themed area after another, building up their anticipation." Adrian Fisher and Georg Gerster, The Art of the Maze, pg. 85.

the hero's journeys undertaken by Neo in the *Matrix*, Luke Skywalker in *Star Wars*, and Frodo in *The Lord of the Rings*.

Architecture has also felt the influence of the labyrinth—in New York City you can bear witness to Frank Lloyd Wright's masterpiece The Guggenheim Museum, an upside down spiraling Babylonian temple. You begin your visit at the museum on the top of the building and make your way down a gently—sloping continuous ramp,[3] where each "space flows freely one into another."

So you get the idea—a *laberinto* is old and it's been around. Almost like certain marketing campaigns—but in this case, saturation did not diminish its value.

This book is meant to bring the secrets and power of the *laberinto* into your professional life. It is divided into three parts. Part I covers Chapters 1–3 and gives you a brief history of the *laberinto*, where it comes from, the myths associated with it and how they relate to business today. Part II consists of Chapter 4, which describes how to use the *laberintos* provided in this book and Chapter 5, which contains 16 *laberintos* focusing on business topics (including marketing, human resource management, leadership, etc.) plus 1 bonus *laberinto* on business wisdom. Part III concludes the book with *laberinto* templates and a reference listing.

So if you are ready, let's begin…

---

3. http://www.guggenheim.org/the_building.html

1

The Myth & the Bull

But where does the *labertino* come from originally? Although it is almost omnipresent tracing it back to its origin is a little complex. Why? *Laberintos* did not exist in ancient times the way that we recognize them today. They were not "places" but representations of concepts. Let me explain by using the story that we most associate with an original labyrinth: the Labyrinth of King Minos of Crete. He was the king who imprisoned the Minotaur, a half-man, half-bull creature (who was his stepson), in a "labyrinth" Every nine years King Minos required Athens to send 7 young boys and 7 young girls to be offered as tribute. These children were then put into the labyrinth where the minotaur would dispose of them. The story continues that the son of the King of Athens, Theseus, volunteers to be sent in tribute. The daughter of King Minos, Ariadne, sees Theseus, falls in love with him and gives him a golden ball of thread to find his way out of the labyrinth. Theseus battles and kills the Minotaur in the labyrinth and escapes by following Ariadne's Thread.

Besides King Minos, Theseus, Ariadne and the Minotaur there are some other peripheral characters integral to the understanding of a *laberinto*—these are Pasiphaë (King Minos' wife), the god Poseidon, Daedalus (the inventor), and his son Icarus.

The story goes that King Minos insulted the god Poseidon by not sacrificing a white bull to him because it was so beautiful the King decided to keep it. As retribution, Poseidon curses Mino's wife Parsiphaë with a passion for the animal. Daedalus arranges for Pasiphaëe to be with the bull and she conceived the Minotaur. King Minos then requests Daedalus to build a prison for the Minotaur, so Daedalus builds the labyrinth. When King Minos discovers Daedalus part in Parsiphaë's betrayal, he had Daedalus and his son Icarus imprisoned in the labyrinth. As Daedalus was an inventor he created wings of feathers and wax so he and his son could escape. As they flew out of the labyrinth, Daedalus warned his son not to fly too close to the sun. Icarus, feeling empowered by flight, did not heed his father's warning and continued to fly upward until the sun melted the wax causing the wings to detach. Icarus falls to his death crashing into the sea.

The legend has existed for over two thousand years. But is it true? We know that King Minos did exist. There is plenty of historical evidence including the rediscovery of his palace at Knossos on the island of Crete in Greece. He was a king, quite tyrannical, and this is what is personified in the legend. However, no remnants of a labyrinth have ever been found where the palace stands. What is found is a magnificent fresco depicting an act of bull-jumping. The athletes are men and women and the fresco dates from the 15th Century BC.

Bulls played an important role in Cretan religion and were associated with the sun. They are strong animals and inspire strong deeds. It is speculated that the "minotaur," a hybrid of bull and human, is symbolic of the connection between man and his god. The leaping over the bull could indicate a "leap of faith" into the unknown or to face an uncertainty. It can also be seen as a metaphor for overcoming obstacles. But it is a physical act, a deliberate decision of movement and timing[1]. Here is our **second lesson from the *laberinto*. We must make *decisions of actions* to be successful**. There is risk in leaping over a bull. There is risk in pursuing new business endeavors. But the thrill of having survived and thrived can be equated with the feeling of divine ecstasy.

The minotaur can also symbolize a past that must be hidden. No matter what we do, evidence is always left behind. In today's digital age your past is never forgotten. So we try to hide it. With each new position we start with a new blank slate. We can reinvent ourselves to be better than our past. But the past

---

1.　This website contains QuickTime movies of bull dancing and modern day bull leaping. Enjoy. http://www.marin.cc.ca.us/~jim/photos/bullstuff/bulldance.html

always lurks there. Think about your past positions. Anything you wouldn't want your current colleagues to know about? How do you hide it? Stuffed in a show box at the bottom of the closet? What did King Minos need to hide? His god cursed him, his wife betrayed him, he had an ugly stepson stronger than him, and all he got was a white bull! Interesting is that King Minos hid it in plain sight. Everyone knew of the labyrinth and the minotaur. It became part of the culture.

At the end of the day though, the minotaur is discovered and destroyed. "And the truth shall set you free!" Yes, **the third lesson. What is the secret you are hiding?** Why are you hiding it? You will have to face that secret eventually—in the center of the *laberinto* or in the center of your home, in the bottom of the closet. For in the end, as you will discover, the minotaur is yourself.

Did the minotaur exist? It is accepted that minotaurs and other animal-human hybrid creatures did not exist although they are revered as gods and goddesses (think Egypt and Sumeria). So where did the image come from? Could it be something as innocent as a foreign visitor witnessing bull leaping for the first time from a fair distance and assuming that the bull and the leaper were one? When the Spaniards arrived in South and Central America riding their horses they were assumed to be a horse-man hybrid. So this is a possible explanation. **Lesson 4: Don't always believe what you see.**

Regardless of its reality, the minotaur, as a bull and as itself, has attained a firm place in modern imagination. Pablo Picasso had an obsession with it, depicting the minotaur in various sketches and painting throughout his career. Drinking Minotaur and Reclining Woman, Minotaur Attacking an Amazon, The Office Party, Minotaur with a Javelin and Woman Hostage, Minotaur defeated, Minotauromachy, Composition with Minotaur, Still Life with Minotaur Head, are just a few.[2] Picasso used different styles to depict the minotaur—some in color, some just black and white. He also portrayed the minotaur in different roles—as a predator, a lover, an office worker, a defeated monster and a triumphant artist. What was Picasso trying to tell us? What was

---

2. You can look these up on the Internet to see what they look like. Many poster websites and art gallery websites offer thumbnail images that can be enlarged.

he looking for in his variations of the minotaur? What do we see when we look at his depictions? Here is another lesson. **Lesson 5: See, don't just look.**

To summarize: King Minos represents tyrannical authority and the minotaur represents a hidden secret. What about Theseus and Ariadne? Next chapter please...

2

The Hero's Journey

We are up to Theseus—the hero of the story. Theseus volunteers to be sacrificed, slays the Minotaur, gets the girl and escapes. Simple enough. He is doing what every hero has done and will do in every hero story ever made. But why? Why is he doing it at all? What makes a person wake up one morning and decide to put his/her life and everything he/she knows and has at risk to complete some quest that they did not even have to be involved with?

Joseph Campbell was born on March 26, 1904 in New York. Little did he know that his interest in Native American myths and culture would turn into a life-long obsession with world myths and their meaning in the modern world. Campbell would become the best-known comparative mythologist of his time offering books, lectures and a six-part television interview to disseminate his views on myths and particularly the role of the hero[1]. Campbell believed that myths were essential and necessary as they provide instruction on how to live. His seminal work was published in 1949: <u>The Hero with a Thousand Faces</u>. As Campbell was influenced by Carl Jung and James Joyce, his work would influence generations of Hollywood producers, among them Christopher Vogler from Disney, who would summarize Campbell's journey into 12 steps followed closely by George Lucas for his *Star Wars* films[2].

---

1.   *The Power of Myth* with Bill Moyers, 1987.
2.   There are many websites that offer in-depth analysis of how the hero's journey is depicted in Star Wars. Feel free to enter "Star Wars" and "Joseph Campbell" or "hero's journey" into a search engine. You'll be surprised as to what comes up.

Volger's twelve steps are reduced from Campbell's original thirteen. Looking for more simplicity I came upon Reg Harris's and Susan Thompson's version with only eight[3].

Campbell[4]	Volger	Harris/Thompson
Part I. Departure		*Part I. Separation*
	Ordinary World	
The Call to Adventure	Call to Adventure	The Call
Refusal of the Call	Refusal of the Call	
Supernatural Aid	Meeting with the Mentor	
The Crossing of the First Threshold	Crossing the First Threshold	The Threshold
The Belly of the Whale		
Part II. Initiation		*Part II. Initiation & Transformation*
The Road of Trials	Tests/Allies/Enemies	The Challenges
The Meeting with the Goddess		The Abyss
Woman as Temptress		
Atonement with the Father	Approach	The Transformation
Apotheosis	Supreme Ordeal	The Revelation
The Ultimate Boon	Reward	The Atonement

---

3. *The Hero's Journey: Life's Great Adventure* http://www.yourheroicjourney.com/Journey.shtml
4. For a good description of each of these steps in detail look at Alan Levine's *The Hero's Journey: Summary of Steps* http://www.mcli.dist.maricopa.edu/smc/journey/ref/summary.html

Part III. Return		**Part III. The Return**
Refusal of the Return		
The Magic Flight	The Return Back	
Rescue from Without		
The Crossing of the Return Threshold	Resurrection	
Master of Two Worlds		
Freedom to Live	Return with the Elixir	The Return (with a gift)

Table 1: Hero's Journey Comparisons

When put side by side we see that Volger's and Harris's journeys have combined a few of Campbell's steps. What Volger has added is a new first step before the Call to Adventure—the Ordinary World. This is important and Campbell seems to have taken this for granted. But we must understand what the ordinary world is before we can attempt to transform it in any way. If we do not see it correctly then we will not know what, if anything, needs to be changed at all—whether within ourselves, our companies, our world.

The other thing Volger did was eliminate categorizing the steps. For him they compile one list, not three; it is one journey with no pauses or rest stops. In this too we can understand Volger's refusal to dangle in superficial divisions. Remember also, Volger's purpose was to create a mechanism—a template—for adventure films—not to provide a comprehensive review of world mythology—Campbell had already done that.

Back to Theseus and the labertinto. How does all this connect? And what is its relevance to our business success? **Lesson 6 of the *laberinto*: Be patient.** It takes time to walk the laberinto and it takes time to find the answers/solutions you seek. And then once found it takes time to implement them and see the results.

Campbell, Volger and Harris/Thompson also assume that the hero is chosen already. But who is the hero chosen? Is it voluntary (like Theseus), is it because of circumstances (like Luke Skywalker) or is it just fate/destiny (like Neo from *The Matrix*)? As you review the steps listed below ask yourself—are you the hero? Why or why not? If you are not the hero who is? Does it have to be you (in the case of a business issue) or can someone else be the hero—someone better prepared perhaps? Do you want to be the hero? Why or why not?

Volger	Theseus	*Laberinto*
Ordinary World	King Minos is taking the tribute of 14 young people and killing them by means of the Minotaur every 9 years.	The current market scenario for your product/service or you; including: competitors, technology, marketing, etc.
Call to Adventure	Theseus believes that something should be done to stop it.	Something has happened in your business/life that necessitates a change; a "crisis." What is that crisis? Where, or from whom, did it come from?
Refusal of the Call	Theseus never questions what he should do (at least the myths does not indicate that he doubts) and so he offers himself as part of the sacrifice.	You may not be sure how to proceed or even if you should. Should you try the *laberinto* or not?
Meeting with the Mentor	Theseus mentor is Ariadne, King Mino's daughter. She gives Theseus a talisman—a charm of good luck to remind him to stay his course—it is a ball of golden thread.	Who are your mentors in your professional/personal life? Yes, there can be more than one. They can also just be helpers in your journey. Where did you find them or did they find you? How? In this book, I will be your guide in the *laberinto*—you will follow my Ariadne's Thread through the process. What is you talisman? Only you know.

Crossing the First Threshold	Theseus leaves Athens bound on the ship that will make him a sacrifice. This is the point of no return, when the decision is made to go forward no matter what may happen. Interesting that in Theseus story the crossing occurs before the meeting with his mentor.	Who are the guardians in your company? What are they guarding? Why is it so difficult to get through them to reach where you need to go to resolve the business situation? Or is the question—why are you afraid to step over the threshold? What is holding you back? Or have you made the decision already?
Tests/Allies/Enemies	Theseus meets Ariadne who also serves as Campbell's goddess. King Minos is happy to see his opponent's son as a sacrifice. Theseus enters the labyrinth and starts to make his way toward the center.	Who are your allies at your job? Your enemies? What tests, obstacles, challenges do you face each day at work? Sometimes this is known as "paying your dues." What temptations are you faced with? What are you learning from your interactions? How do they make you stronger? Wiser?
Approach	With every turn Theseus lets the thread lose creating a pathway back.	Every day at your job you make your way—sometimes with small steps, sometimes with larger steps. What are you making your way too? Do you know what your destination it? How do you know you are reaching it?

Supreme Ordeal	Theseus encounters the minotaur and after a battle kills him.	You have reached the center of the *laberinto*. You have reached the boundary between what you want and actually having it. What do you see? What do you need to do to reach it? Who must you confront (or at least prove yourself to for the promotion, etc.)? What is your ultimate challenge at your job/business? This is where you face it.
Reward	Theseus is alive.	You have reached the center. You reach your goal. In doing so you have been transformed by your ordeal. The lessons become revelations that you internalize as wisdom to pass on. You have, as they say in business, a "paradigm shift."
The Return Back	Theseus, with the other sacrificial youths in tow, follow the golden thread back out.	You survived the encounter—but what does it all mean? As you work your way out of the *laberinto* you reflect on your journey and internalize the lessons learned—you "atone" as Campbell would say. To atone means to make "one with." You accept the new "you" and understand that the old "you" is dead and must be left behind. This can be old habits, old business, old customers, old colleagues. Anything that would not allow you to move forward. Your grieving period for these things left behind is over. You feel lighter and are ready for the next stage.

Resurrection	Theseus exits the labyrinth.	You survived and end your journey in the *laberinto*. You step out of it (or in this case, you finish your last reflection). Was it successful? Was it worth it? Only you can answer that.
Return with the Elixir	Theseus leaves Crete with Ariande.	"What do you choose to bring back to the world after your journey?"[5] Is it a gift of understanding or a gift of a promotion? Just as important is how do others respond to the "new" you, the one who got the gift? How do you respond with their response?

Table 2: Volger/Theseus/Laberinto Analysis

One last thing, in case you were wondering, apparently Theseus was based on a real individual as his name was found on ancient tablets indicating he was a leader of Athens and may have even sailed with Jason and the Argonauts. This guy got around.

To end this chapter, I would like to leave you with another version of the Hero's Journey. This one is in the form of a poem by Mary Oliver, Pulitzer Prize winning poet born in Ohio, USA. It is one of the components compiled in a study guide of the hero's journey by Karen Wurl of Kennesaw State University entitled *The Hero's Journey, Mythic Stories of the Hero's Quest.*[6]

---

5. Helen Curry, The Way of the Labyrinth, pg. 97
6. This study guide was a companion website to the *2004 Mythic Journeys Conference* which celebrated the centennial of Joseph Campbells birth. http://www.kennesaw.edu/theatre/StudyGuides/Hero-Journey/index-hj.html

The Journey

One day you finally knew
what you had to do, and began,
though the voices around you
kept shouting
their bad advice—
though the whole house
began to tremble
and you felt the old tug
at your ankles.
"Mend my life!"
each voice cried.
But you didn't stop.
You knew what you had to do,
though the wind pried
with its stiff fingers
at the very foundations,
though their melancholy
was terrible.
It was already late
enough, and a wild night,
and the road full of fallen
branches and stones.
But little by little,
as you left their voices behind,
the stars began to burn
through the sheets of clouds,
and there was a new voice
which you slowly
recognized as your own,
that kept you company
as you strode deeper and deeper

into the world,
determined to do
the only thing you could do—
determined to save
the only life you could save.

—*Mary Oliver*

3

Alchemy/Transformation

We go through the *laberinto* but do we understand what happens to us in the process? There are many descriptions of what occurs to the pilgrim once he/she reaches the center. Or at least descriptions of what is supposed to occur. In its most fundamental form, the center of the *laberinto* is an encounter with oneself. Many labyrinth-walking experts and labyrinth-walkers themselves will emphasize how important it is to reach the center—the goal by continuing to follow the path of the labyrinth. But when using the *laberinto* the important thing for you will be the journey—and what happens in the journey—the transformation. And when you speak of transformation, another ancient art demands to be explored—alchemy.

The word alchemy usually conjures up images of wizards and old wise men trying to find the secret of turning base medals—like lead—into gold. This is what makes it important for business; gold = profits/success. The secret is called the *philosopher's stone*, and the process is called *Opus*, The Great Work. In truth, alchemy heralds from ancient Egypt and reaches medieval Europe through the Arabs and Chinese. It is a chemical process of working with elements at their primary qualities to alter them in such a way that they will reconfigure into something more than they were before. It is not so far fetched if we look at today's technology and its use in understanding physics and the structure of atoms and particles.[1]

---

1. Another way to think about this is through Carl Sagan's belief that "we are all made of star stuff" celestial particles that have drifted to earth to create life on this planet by being refined to the point that humans were born.

We need to view alchemy as synonymous with "transformation", or "change". After all that is what we want in our business—to effect change to reach success.

True alchemy interrelates religion with science, taking tangible matter and infusing it with concepts of spiritual purification. In fact, according to Carl Jung[2], the renown psychoanalyst, the alchemist were the true discoverers of the subconscious, and what they were trying to achieve was divine perfection in themselves—they wanted to change themselves into gold. They did this by experimentation—physical with the elements and spiritual with themselves.

To better illustrate let's take a look at the seven stages of the alchemical process[3]

Stage	Color	Animal	Description
Calcinatio	Black	Crow/Raven	The use of fire to heat a substance getting it to its core elements.
Solutio	White	Swan/Eagle	Dissolving any unrefined particles in a liquid.
Separatio	Green	Lion	Separating the elements into distinct and purified base forms. An analysis can now take place.
Coniunctio	Various Colors	Peacock's Tail	The fusing of the elements in new combinations to create a new substance.

2. It was Carl Jung who influenced Joseph Campbell and his theories on mythology and the *hero's journey*. See Chapter 2.

3. After much research, I discovered that the stages can be sequences in different orders, adding to the complexity that the alchemists found themselves in—not only what materials to heat, mix, separate and solidify, but also in what order could effect the outcome of their experiments. Also, the table is a compilation of different theories of alchemy and is used here for illustrative purposes only. The animal symbolism is adapted from *Animal Symbolism in the Alchemical Tradition*, by Adam McLean http://www.alchemywebsite.com

Sublimatio	White	Unicorn	The distilling of the new substance through fire to bring it to a higher level of purity; making it into a gas.
Coagulatio	Red	Pelican	The new substance is made solid through the introduction of a coagulating substance (i.e. blood).
Mortificatio	Flaming Red	Phoenix	The death of the original substance and its rebirth as something completely new

Table 3: Seven Stages of the Alchemical Process

It is interesting to note that some well-known scientists, Sir Isaac Newton, for instance would spend half of his life's work investigating and experimenting with alchemy. His family would burn most of his notes on the subject after his death, wrongfully believing that the notes served as damning evidence against Newton's scientific credibility. Sir Francis Bacon was another hidden alchemist. You should remember Bacon. He is quoted as saying "Knowledge is power." Perhaps he had found this power in alchemy.

This brings us back to Carl Jung. "Jungarian" approach to psychotherapy relies on the interpretation of dreams as the messengers of our subconscious. In other words, our dreams tell us what we can not tell ourselves when we are wide awake. The problem is, dreams are given to us in symbolic language—nothing is what it seems[4]—and so we need help to interpret them to better understand ourselves. Jung believed in this so much that when he dreamed about an ancient library full of old and arcane books, he spent 15 years building it and collecting the books to fill it. Many of these old books were about alchemy and hence begins Jung's fascination with the old science. As he reads his books, he begins to translate the symbols used and discovers a relation between the external chemical experiments and the internal purification process of the alchemist. Jung publishes his revelations in three major volumes: <u>Alchemical Studies</u>, <u>Psychology and Alchemy</u>, and <u>Mysterium Coniunctionis</u>. (*I'd like to see you try saying that three times fast!*)

---

4. For example, a dream of a wedding supposedly forewarns of a death of someone close to the dreamer.

So how did Jung correlate alchemy and psychology and how does it relate to our *laberinto*? Because of his focus on symbolism it is appropriate that we use his theory for our understanding of the transformation that occurs in a *laberinto*.

Jung Stage of Transformation based on Nigel Hamilton[5]	Meaning	Laberinto
Nigredo/Blackening	This is the encounter with the darker aspects of ourselves—what Jung called the "shadow." Because most of this shadow is subconscious, it can feel chaotic and not pleasant. Confusion sets in. Most people want to escape from this and would rather not look deep inside to heal or correct what may be wrong. This stage is related to the concept of "earth"—the possession of material things and the social world (position, employment, etc.) To move to the next step a person must let go of the old sense of self.	You begin the *laberinto* because there is something you need to resolve—sometimes it is something you do not want to face because you do not know how. As you walk the *laberinto* you know you will have to face it—there is no where else to go, you must proceed forward. This step also asks you to start to answer the difficult questions—who are you? How do you identify yourself? Are you just your position? Are you just what you possess? What are your attachments that relate to the issue you need resolved? What emotions are getting in the way? You need a clear head.

5. To put this table together I relied on Nigel Hamilton's *The Alchemical Process of Transformation*, 1985 http://www.sufismus.ch/omega_dream/alchemy_e.pdf and Iona Miller's *Introduction to Alchemy in Jungarian Psychology*, 1986 http://zero-point.tripod.com/alchemy/alchemyclass.html

Albedo/Whitening	This is the encounter of the lighter aspects of our-selves—our gifts and special qualities. Now that the "bad" stuff has been removed we can appreciate the "good" stuff we have to offer. This stage is related to the concept of the "moon." It is a lonely stage and can be evidenced by a period of withdrawing. We need to inter-nalize what we have learned.	Now that you know what is involved in the problem/opportunity/ issue at hand—includ-ing the who and the what—you can think about what resources *are* available to you to resolve this issue. You can be creative; you may discover new tal-ents and skills you had or new resources and contacts you may not have thought of before because of all the emo-tions you were drown-ing in.
Citrinitas/Yellowing	This is the encounter with a rev-elation of ourselves. We receive the inner knowledge—an insight into ourselves that is immediate and direct. This stage is related to the concept of the "sun" as a source of light and life. Pure illu-mination.	You have reached the center of the *laberinto* or its end and know the answer. In fact, it could come at any moment on your journey. It comes suddenly, almost like a jolt and you wonder why you did not think of it before. But you know it is per-fect. You feel elated, relieved and light.

Rubedo/Reddening	This is the encounter with the real world after the personal revelation. Related to the concept of "returning to earth." Changes in personality have taken affect because of the insights gained and the effort this requires is substantial.	You have the answer. Now you must implement it. For some this is the hard part as there is no guarantee that your "perfect" solution will be "perfect" for everyone involved. Habits are hard to break, especially bad business practices. You *must* exit the *laberinto*; nothing can be achieved until you leave its safe haven.

Table 4: Jung and Laberinto Correlations

At this point we can finish with the Theseus and Minotaur myth by examining the last two characters—Daedalus and Icarus—father and son. Daedalus was an inventor. To invent implies the act of experimenting with what does and does not work, so we can call Daedalus an alchemist to a certain extent. He was faced with a serious problem—how to save himself and his son, Icarus, from being killed and eaten by the Minotaur. To do that Daedalus had to find a way out of the labyrinth, they had to escape. He thinks and comes up with the solution of wings. Using the materials at hand Daedalus makes them and presents it to Icarus. They fly out.

The solution worked beautifully, except that Icarus did not stop. Could Daedalus have foreseen the reaction of Icarus to his new power? Could Daedalus have countered the effect of such liberty on his son? Could Daedalus prevent his son's death? No. All he could do was try. How many times have we tried to prevent someone from making a big mistake and then they make a bigger one? The moral is that the alchemical process is an individual one. What gets released has a life of its own. Icarus had his own transformation to go through but did not go through it because his father did it for him. And as we see from the myth, that never works. Flying high is an amazing feeling—one of the reasons we enjoy parachuting, or roller coasters, or even hiking or climbing a mountain to its peak. We feel above the others, superior, that we see the big picture and no one else has to be concerned with it—just do as we say to do, no questions asked. Many a leader or manager in a business has discovered that this approach does not always provide the results they think it will. **Lesson 7: Power without wisdom is no power at all.**

One last question—alchemy is all about the great work, the Opus—what is your great work? What is your Opus? If you don't know what it is, then how do you know you are not wasting your time? **Lesson 8: Know your Opus.**

4

Using the Laberintos

With all that background foundation out of the way, we are ready for the final instructions on how to use the 17 business *laberintos* provided for you in Chapter 5.

The first step, as in any business endeavor, is preparation. You need to prepare yourself for the journey. First, do you have the time to spend in this mental exercise? Give yourself from 30-45 minutes per *laberinto* at least. Are you in a tranquil place, free of distractions? Some individuals like to listen to calming music while they experience the *laberinto*—classical, soft jazz, Gregorian chants or music from the Medieval or Renaissance time periods. Is the lighting correct for your mood? Do you prefer natural light from outside or soft lamp light or candles? Are you comfortable? Clothes not too tight? Tie off? Heels stashed under the desk? Sofa, chair offering good support? Temperature ok? Not too cold not too hot? Do you have what you need? A pen or pencil, extra sheets of blank paper, the *laberinto* book?

Take out the *laberinto* templates from the back of the book. Select a personal marker to help you progress your journey. The marker can be anything, but it should have some personal significance to you. You can use a crystal, a piece of jewelry, a coin, a company pin, a monopoly game piece, a paperclip. As longs as you know what it means, you can use it. It is now your talisman.

Now, ask yourself about your intentions. What do you want to achieve today? What has been on your mind? What issues need to be resolved?

Turn to Chapter 5 and read through the list of business *laberintos*. Which one(s) speaks out to you? Select it. (You do not have to go in order to get the full effect of the laberintos). Put your marker on Station 1 and begin the *laberinto*.

Think of yourself as a pilgrim on a quest, but instead of going to the Holy Land, you are reaching the land of prosperity and business success.

Each laberinto consists of 22 stations; 10 going in, 2 in the center (both numbered 11), and 10 going out. Each station is correlated to a word used as a symbol. You are given the symbol, a quote used as a description of the symbol, a comment to help you focus on the quote and space to write down your reflections of the quote or your answers to the questions asked in the comments. Move your marker to each subsequent station as you progress through the *laberinto*.

When you exit (finish) the *laberinto* take a few moments to remember your experience and your emotional reactions to the stations. Now ask yourself: what do you want to take back with you from this experience? What do you want to share and release to your business? How will this gain you success? Take these new perspectives and insights and apply them. Do it. **Lesson 9: Begin.**

A few things to remember while doing this work:

1. It is work, it takes effort. If you feel that just reading the quotes and comments will bring you the success you desire, you are sadly mistaken. The process is also not done with your reflections. The work is only completed once you implement the insights obtained—and that takes a lot more work on your part.

2. Shed any expectations that you may have about the process. Open your mind to any surprises that may come your way. This can take the shape of questions, images in your mind, snippets of songs or movie clips, even memories of something that you feel has no connection whatsoever with your focus. But it came to you. Accept it. Move on.

3. Go at your own pace. This is why I say you need to make sure you have enough time. You do not want to rush the process. But take it at your leisure so the "wisdom" can sink in. Pause if you need to. Stop altogether if it is becoming too overwhelming. Just remember where you left off with the personal marker and pick it up again. You should not leave a laberinto unfinished for too long a time. Then you will lose the advantage of what you learned and gained in the previous stations.

4. Be conscious of the process and then let go. This can be a kinetic exercise if you want to include walking, breathing, etc. But most importantly you need to "be" in the process—it is a deliberate choice you made to undertake this laberinto.

5. For some, walking the *laberinto* is a struggle as they do not enjoy the realities they begin to face to resolve their issues (see Chapter 3 Alchemy). This is because the laberinto is "a place of contradiction: hope and fear, beauty and danger.[1]" Anything can happened and we are not always welcoming of the unknown, especially in business. You need to learn to trust the process, and more importantly, to trust yourself.

6. You will notice that as you move the marker you sometimes come close to the center and then are sent far away from it again. This is to symbolize that you learn more by going around the goal then what you learn in a quick, one-time success. You need patience to nurture the success to make it lasting. The difference between being prosperous and being rich can sometimes be how long you keep the wealth.

7. Another truth in the circular path of the *laberinto* is that you have to learn to accept that sometimes you must take a turn back, a turn around, in order to proceed ahead. Progress is not a straight line and neither is success.

8. Another metaphor to be used from the symbolism of the *laberinto* is that when we walk it we are walking in the "empty" space between its "walls" (lines). That is because the boundaries are immaterial. What

---

1. Virginia Westby, <u>Labyrinths: Ancient Paths</u>, page 9.

is important is that we can "fill" the empty space with ourselves, our thoughts, our insights.

These *laberintos* are an opportunity for you for self-discovery and self-defini-tion in terms of your professional career, your business and your future success. But at the end, as in the center, what you will find is yourself. A different self from the person who began the journey, but still yourself. Accept and embrace this new self which brings with it the resolutions you seek. **Lesson 10: End.**

5

Business Laberintos

1. Business Leaders

2. Business Wisdom (1)

3. Human Resource Management

4. Business strategy

5. Consumer Service/Satisfaction

6. Marketing

7. Creativity and Innovation

8. Leadership

9. Negotiation

10. Business Wisdom (2)

11. International Business

12. Technology

Laberinto #1
Business Leaders

Going In

Station	Direction	Symbol	Description/Reflection
1	In	Bill Gates, CEO of Microsoft	Take our 20 best people away and I will tell you that Microsoft would become an unimportant company. (1996)
		Comment:	Are companies supposed to be important? Why? Who are they important to? Is your company important? Why? Who is it important to? What or who makes it important? Do you agree with Bill? Why or why not?
		Reflection:	_____ _____ _____
2	Curve	Lee Iacocca	Mistakes are a part of life; you can't avoid them. All you can hope is that they won't be too expensive and that you don't make the same mistake twice. (1984)
		Comment:	Think about a mistake you have done that you keep carrying around with you. What did you learn? Let it go and move on. Think about a mistake someone on your team made and you keep carrying it around with you. What did you learn? Let it go and move on.
		Reflection:	_____ _____ _____

3	Curve	Alfred P. Sloan	There is no resting place for an enterprise in a competitive economy.
		Comment:	Complacency is a vice. Your competitors continue to compete. Being number one is not guaranteed to last unless you work at maintaining it. Are you complacent with what you or your company has achieved? How can you achieve more?
		Reflection:	_____ _____ _____
4	Curve	Aristotle Onassis	The secret of business is to know something that nobody else knows.
		Comment:	What do you know that makes you valuable to your company?
		Reflection:	_____ _____ _____
5	Curve	Woodrow Wilson	If you want to make enemies, try to change something.
		Comment:	Change brings with it work and people are resistant to anything that adds to their burdens. They feel they are working hard enough already. They are comfortable with how things are. What have you changed or tried to change lately? Why did you want it changed? If you have not changed anything, why not? What is holding you back?
		Reflection:	_____ _____ _____
6	Curve	Rupert Murdoch	The buck stops with the guy who signs the check.

		Comment:	Accountability and responsibility go hand in hand. What are you not taking accountability for? Why not? Is it truly your responsibility? If not, who does it belong to? Give it back.
		Reflection:	_____ _____ _____
7	Bend	Coco Channel	In order to be irreplaceable, one must always be different.
		Comment:	What makes you different from everyone else in your team? Your company? Is it a good difference that you can maximize on or is it detrimental to your success?
		Reflection:	_____ _____ _____
8	Curve	Andy Warhol	Being good in business is the most fascinating kind of art. Making money is art, and working is art, and good business is art. (1987)
		Comment:	You can take pride in being a businessperson. It is a noble profession that can make big differences in the world—for example Bill Gate's Foundation has over $35 billion in assets and pursues cures in AIDS, Malaria and substandard education. Are you good at what you do or just good enough? Why?
		Reflection:	_____ _____ _____
9	Bend	David Kearns, Xerox	We realize that we are in a race without a finish line. As we improve so does our competition.

		Comment:	You reach the end of one assignment and another comes up. New issues every day. How can you make this new one better than the last?
		Reflection:	
10	Curve	Dr. Michael Hammer	Every company has its own language, its own version of its own history (its myths) and its own heroes and villains (legends), both historical and contemporary.
		Comment:	What is the corporate culture at your company? What are its stories, who are the heroes and villains, what is their moral? Who would know these things? Find out.
		Reflection:	
11	Center	Steven Spielberg	I dream for a living.
		Comment:	What do you do for a living? Not for money to pay the bills but for living your dreams?
		Reflection:	

Coming Out

Station	Direction	Symbol	Description/Reflection
11	Center	Andrew Carnegie	Mr. Morgan buys his partners; I grow my own. (1932)
		Comment:	How do you make alliances? Why do people want to ally with you? Who do you want to ally with? Why? How can you do it?
		Reflection:	_____ _____ _____
12	Bend	Andrew Grove, CEO, Intel	With all due respect to Microsoft and Intel, there is no substitute for being in the right place at the right time. (1993)
		Comment:	Are you in the right place at the right time when you need to be? Why or why not? How can you fine tune your timing? What do you need?
		Reflection:	_____ _____ _____
13	Bend	Peter Drucker	Edison didn't invent the light bulb…Edison invented the electric industry. (1996)
		Comment:	Are you just selling a product or service or are you creating a new way of living a life?
		Reflection:	_____ _____ _____
14	Curve	G. Richard Thoman, CEO, IBM	The art of management is about choice.

		Comment:	What choices have you made recently? Were they good or bad choices? What determines a good or bad choice? How can you make better choices in the future?
		Reflection:	_____ _____ _____
15	Curve	Louis Ger-stner Jr., CEO, IBM	Just fragmenting an organization does not create conditions sufficient for success.
		Comment:	One small step is one small step—it must be followed by others. What have you started but left unfin-ished? Why? Was it just a fad or trend? What needs to be finished?
		Reflection:	_____ _____ _____
16	Curve	Warren Buffet	One's objective should be to get it right, get it quick, get it out and get it over. You see, your problem won't improve with age. (1995)
		Comment:	What are you holding on to instead of resolving? Why? Do you need to release it to someone else? Why don't you?
		Reflection:	_____ _____ _____
17	Bend	Donald Trump	You just have to be the kind of guy to get people to do things. (1987)
		Comment:	Do people in your company do things for you? Why or why not? If no, how can you improve this? How about suppliers? Do they do things for you? Why or why not?

		Reflection:	_____
18	Curve	Philip H. Knight, CEO, Nike	Once you let people in your office, they'll come in and out all day long. I need to think.
		Comment:	You want to let people know they can communicate with you, but you also need to set your limits. When do you think? Do you have a specific time that you can be left alone? A specific place? Why do you need to think? Why is it so important?
		Reflection:	_____
19	Bend	Bernie Marcus, CEO, Home Depot	This is a basic and simple business. People create problems by not trusting their own judgment. By constantly needing validation. You guys are empowered. You can find 99% of the answers in the aisles where the customers are.
		Comment:	What answers are you looking for when it comes to your customers? Have you asked them? Why or why not?
		Reflection:	_____
20	Curve	Howard Schultze, CEO, Starbucks	Hire people smarter than you and get out of their way.
		Comment:	Who do you surround yourself with? Who do you hire? Why? Can they bring you and your company up or do they just do the job?

		Reflection:	_____ _____ _____
21	Out	Lawrence Bossidy	You can influence people, you can influence your strategy, and you can influence operations. In my judgment, that's all you do.
		Comment:	Who or what do you influence at your company? Who influences you? Who do you want to influence? Who do you not want to have influence over you?
		Reflection:	_____ _____ _____

Laberinto #2
Business Wisdom (1)

Going In

Station	Direction	Symbol	Description/Reflection
1	In	Experience	All truly wise thoughts have been thought already thousands of times; but to make them truly ours, we must think them over again honestly, till they take root in our personal experience. Johann Wolfgang von Goethe
		Comment:	What "truth" have you learned that you can think about in a new way? Does the "truth" of it change?
		Reflection:	_____ _____ _____
2	Curve	Beyond Knowledge	Knowledge is merely brilliance in the organization of ideas. It is not true wisdom. The truly wise go beyond knowledge. Confucius
		Comment:	How do you go beyond the knowledge that is presented to you each day in your business?
		Reflection:	_____ _____ _____
3	Curve	Stubborn	But all the wisdom in heaven has a hard task to overcome the pride of an obstinate scholar. Ancient Sanskrit Verse
		Comment:	Think about a time that you refused to be wrong even though you were? Why? How much trouble could you have saved yourself if you would have had an open mind?

		Reflection:	
4	Curve	Enemies	Wise men learn many things from their enemies. Aristophanes
		Comment:	What can you learn from your competitors? What can you learn from those in your company who are against you?
		Reflection:	
5	Curve	Science	Science is organized knowledge. Wisdom is organized life. Immanuel Kant
		Comment:	What wisdom has your life given you? Write three important things you have learned in the last 3 years?
		Reflection:	
6	Curve	Our Own	We can be knowledgeable with other men's knowledge, but we cannot be wise with other men's wisdom. Michel de Montaigne
		Comment:	Wisdom is personal. What have you learned from someone recently? How did you (how can you) convert this lesson into wisdom?
		Reflection:	
7	Bend	Enough	Finish each day and be done with it. You have done what you could. Ralph Waldo Emerson
		Comment:	What are you taking home with you to bed that should be left behind? Why? Will it change because you relive it?

		Reflection:	_____ _____ _____
8	Curve	Pain	There was never yet philosopher who could endure the toothache patiently. William Shakespeare
		Comment:	Can you understand others' pain or do you try to sweep it away? Do they understand your pain? Why should they if you do not understand theirs?
		Reflection:	_____ _____ _____
9	Bend	Absence	Those who are absent are always wrong. English Proverb
		Comment:	What have you been absent from—meetings, company social events, the office lounge? Do so at your own peril.
		Reflection:	_____ _____ _____
10	Curve	2nd Thoughts	Second thoughts are ever wiser. Euripides
		Comment:	Second thoughts don't count when the event has passed. Learn and move on. What do you have second thoughts about? Why? You can write them in a book and then forget about them until you need them again.
		Reflection:	_____ _____ _____

11	Center	Character	Character cannot be developed in ease and quiet. Only through experience of trial and suffering can the soul be strengthened, vision cleared, ambition inspired, and success achieved. Helen Keller
		Comment:	Experience is messy and sometimes painful. But we learn from what happens to us in our life. Think about a difficult experience you recently had? What did you learn? Could you have avoided it? How?
		Reflection:	_____ _____ _____

Coming Out

Station	Direction	Symbol	Description/Reflection
11	Center	Reversal	What is my turn today may be thine tomorrow. Thomas Fuller
		Comment:	Nothing lasts forever. Who is waiting for your job or position? What job or position are you waiting for? Why are you waiting? Can you do more than just wait?
		Reflection:	_____ _____ _____
12	Bend	Power	We thought because we had power, we had wisdom. Stephen Vincent Benet
		Comment:	What power do you have—authority, etc.? Have you ever abused it by making a decision simply because you could? Why? Would you make that decision now?
		Reflection:	_____ _____ _____
13	Bend	Worth	How much would you be worth if you lost all your money?
		Comment:	Answer this simple question.
		Reflection:	_____ _____ _____
14	Curve	Possibilities	I am unfaithful to my own possibilities when I await from a change of circumstances what I can do on my own initiative. Karl Jaspers
		Comment:	What can I do now? What am I waiting for? Why?

		Reflection:	_____ _____ _____
15	Curve	Simplicity	It is the essence of genius to make use of the simplest ideas. Charles Peguy
		Comment:	What are you making too complicated? How can you simplify it?
		Reflection:	_____ _____ _____
16	Curve	Hard work	Opportunities are usually disguised as hard work so most people don't recognize them. Ann Landers
		Comment:	What opportunities are you missing because they seem like too much additional hard work? Are any of them worth the extra effort? Why or why not?
		Reflection:	_____ _____ _____
17	Bend	$	Watch the costs and the profits will take care of themselves. Andrew Carnegie
		Comment:	You increase income by bringing in more revenue or lowering costs. What costs can you lower—professionally and personally to reach your financial goals?
		Reflection:	_____ _____ _____
18	Curve	Perception	One of the hardest tasks of leadership is understanding that you are not what you are, but what you're perceived to be by others. Edward L. Flom

		Comment:	How do others perceive you? Is it a good image or do you want it changed? What can you do to improve it? Why are you not doing it then? We all care what others think about certain things at some point.
		Reflection:	_____ _____ _____
19	Bend	Prince	A prince who is not himself wise cannot be wisely advised...good advice depends on the shrewdness of the prince who seeks it. Machiavelli, The Prince
		Comment:	Whose advice do you seek? Do you use it? Why or why not? What advice did you not follow that you should have? Why did you not follow it?
		Reflection:	_____ _____ _____
20	Curve	Experience	Good decisions come from wisdom. Wisdom comes from experience. Experience comes from bad decisions. Forbes, 1987
		Comment:	Think about a recent bad decision you made. What were the consequences? What did you learn? Would you make that decision again? Why or why not?
		Reflection:	_____ _____ _____
21	Out	Value	Try not to become a man of success, but rather try to become a man of value. Albert Einstein

		Comment:	What is a person of value? Are you a person of value? What would make you a person of value? What is holding you back from being a person of value?
		Reflection:	_____ _____ _____

Laberinto #3
Human Resource Management

Going In

Station	Direction	Symbol	Description/Reflection
1	In	Cultivate	Small things grow mightily if they are skillfully combined. Blades of grass will make a rope to bind a ranging elephant. Hitopadesha, 14th Century, India
		Comment:	Are the members of your team skillfully combined? Why or why not? How can you make it so?
		Reflection:	_____ _____ _____
2	Curve	Potential	If you find a thing difficult consider whether it would be possible for any person to do it. Because anything that is humanly possible, that falls within human capabilities, you too can accomplish. Marcus Aurelius
		Comment:	Are there those who work on your team that do not believe in themselves? Why? How can you help them believe they can do the task they have been assigned? How can you believe it?
		Reflection:	_____ _____ _____
3	Curve	Right Assignment	A musician must make music, an artist must paint, a poet must write, if he is to be at peace with himself. What a man can be, he must be. Abraham Maslow

		Comment:	Are the employees in your company placed in the right positions for their skills and talents to be fully utilized? Are you in the right place for your own skills and talents to bloom?
		Reflection:	_____ _____ _____
4	Curve	Motivation	Pleasure in the task puts perfection in the work. Aristotle
		Comment:	How would you rate your job satisfaction? How would others in your company rate theirs? Can this be changed? How?
		Reflection:	_____ _____ _____
5	Curve	Age	It is better to be 70 years young than 40 years old. Oliver Wendell Holmes
		Comment:	How old are you? How old do you act? How old are the others on your team? In your office? How old do they act? Are there any patterns here?
		Reflection:	_____ _____ _____
6	Curve	Potential (2)	We have a hunger of the mind which asks for knowledge of all around us and the more we gain, the more is our desire; the more we see, the more we are capable of seeing. Maria Mitchell
		Comment:	Are the employees in your company/ members of your team/getting what they need to know to do their job or to do their best?
		Reflection:	_____ _____ _____

7	Bend	Training	A mind is a fire to be kindled, not a vessel to be filled. Plutarch
		Comment:	What kind of training is offered in your company? Does it sound like corporate propaganda?
		Reflection:	_____
8	Curve	Replacement	Every old man dies is a library that burns. Amadou Hampate Ba
		Comment:	Look around your company. How many are there that you can learn from? Who would you like to learn from? Why? Try to learn something from someone every day.
		Reflection:	_____
9	Bend	Recognition	Deep in their hearts, most people wish to be understood and cherished. The Buddha
		Comment:	How does your company recognize the services of its employees? Is it sufficient? Why or why not? Can you do anything to recognize those on your team?
		Reflection:	_____
10	Curve	Same Team	Once the game is over, the king and pawn go back in the same box. Italian Proverb
		Comment:	Does everyone in the office feel they are on the same team? Why or why not?

		Reflection:	_____
11	Center	Opportunity	One can present people with their opportunities. One cannot make them equal to them. Rosamond Lehmann
		Comment:	Everyone has limits. Are there any on your team that just cannot do what they need to? What can you do to help them reach up or what can you do to help them find another place?
		Reflection:	_____

Coming Out

Station	Direction	Symbol	Description/Reflection
11	Center	Talent	Mediocrity knows nothing higher than itself, but talent instantly recognizes genius. Sir Arthur Conan Doyle
		Comment:	Are the employees in your company talented or skillful or both? What does your company need to reach the next level?
		Reflection:	_____ _____ _____
12	Bend	Ability	It is easier to appear worthy of positions that we have not got than of those that we have. La Rochefoucauld
		Comment:	What is your position? Are you fulfilling that position? What position do you think you can do? Research that position to find out the truth of what it entails? Now that you know more about it can you fulfill it?
		Reflection:	_____ _____ _____
13	Bend	Hiring	New faces have more authority than accustomed ones. Euripides
		Comment:	Does your company promote from within or hire from outside? Why? How do employees react towards a promoted person versus a person completely new in a position of authority? How do you react?
		Reflection:	_____ _____ _____

14	Curve	Beauty	Beauty is a greater recommendation than any letter of introduction. Aristotle
		Comment:	What beauty do you bring to the job? What beauty do others bring to your company?
		Reflection:	_____ _____ _____
15	Curve	Hiring (2)	A great city is not to be confounded with a populous one. Aristotle
		Comment:	Is everyone on your team/in your office/in your company necessary? Why or why not? If not, why are they still there?
		Reflection:	_____ _____ _____
16	Curve	Performance	A man is not good or bad for one action. Thomas Fuller
		Comment:	Bad days happen to everyone and everyone gets lucky every once in a while. Do you determine an employees worth after one mistake or after one success? Why or why not? Look at their track record. What does your track record say about you?
		Reflection:	_____ _____ _____
17	Bend	Belief	The eyes believe themselves, the ears believe other people.
		Comment:	Are you an eye or an ear person? Why?
		Reflection:	_____ _____ _____

18	Curve	Break	Do the employees at a tea factory get coffee breaks?
		Comment:	What is the value of a coffee break? Does your company have coffee breaks? Where is the coffee break held? What is offered at the coffee break? What does the coffee break say about your company?
		Reflection:	_____ _____ _____
19	Bend	Old vs. New	A new broom sweeps clean. But the old one knows where the dirt it.
		Comment:	There are advantages to bringing in new people and there are advantages keeping old employees. What is the trend in your company—do they tend to hire new or promote the old? What do you do?
		Reflection:	_____ _____ _____
20	Curve	Deserve	The employee generally gets the employer he deserves.
		Comment:	And vice-versa. Are you/your company getting what you/it deserves? Why or why not? How can you change this? Do you want to change this? Why or why not?
		Reflection:	_____ _____ _____
21	Out	Goal	Without some goal and some effort to reach it, no man can live. Fyodor Dostoevki

		Comment:	Do the employees in your company know the company's objectives? Do you? What are they? Do you/they have goals you/they must meet? Why or why not?
		Reflection:	_____ _____ _____

Laberinto #4
Business Strategy

Going In

Station	Direction	Symbol	Description/Reflection
1	In	Plans	Our plans fail because they have no aim. For the sailor who does not know where to set his course, there are no favorable winds. Seneca
		Comment:	Where are you going? Where is the company heading to? Why?
		Reflection:	_____ _____ _____
2	Curve	Paths	There are many paths up the mountain, but the view of the moon from the top is the same. Ancient Japanese Saying
		Comment:	Review your strategic plan—have new alternatives (improved technology, new expertise, etc.) come up since you last worked on it? How can you integrate them now?
		Reflection:	_____ _____ _____
3	Curve	Possibilities	It is a world of startling possibilities. Charles Fletcher Pole
		Comment:	What possibilities can you or your company explore? Why or why not?
		Reflection:	_____ _____ _____

4	Curve	Reality	Gold dust is precious, but when it gets in your eyes it blurs your vision. Xitang
		Comment:	Is there gold dust in your eyes or in your company's eyes? What is it and how did it get there? How can you clear your vision?
		Reflection:	_____ _____ _____
5	Curve	Thought	Mind is the great lever of all things; human thought is the process by which human ends are ultimately answered. Daniel Webster
		Comment:	Do you have the best minds of your company working on its strategic plan? Why or why not? Who are the best minds?
		Reflection:	_____ _____ _____
6	Curve	Response	Do not learn how to react, but how to respond. The Buddha
		Comment:	What is the difference between reacting and responding? How can you prepare yourself and your company to respond and not react?
		Reflection:	_____ _____ _____
7	Bend	Simplicity	Simplicity is the ultimate sophistication. Leonardo da Vinci
		Comment:	Is your strategic plan simple enough to be sophisticated? Why or why not? What do you need to do to make it so?

		Reflection:	
8	Curve	Caution	Situations are easier to enter than to exit; but it is common sense to look for the way out before venturing in. Aesop
		Comment:	How do you know your decision is correct? Review your strategic plan and see how the operating plans fulfill it?
		Reflection:	
9	Bend	Priority	Men make holy what he believes as he makes beautiful what he loves. Ernest Renan
		Comment:	What are the priorities for you and your company? Why? Does your strategic plan reflect these priorities? Why or why not? How can you get them aligned?
		Reflection:	
10	Curve	Adaptability	It is not the strongest of the species that survives or the most intelligent. It is the one that is the most adaptable to change. Charles Darwin
		Comment:	How adaptable are you? How adaptable is your company? How adaptable is your strategic plan? How can you make it more adaptable? What is preventing it from being adaptable?
		Reflection:	

11	Center	Arrival	It is not enough for a man to have arrived, it is necessary to know in what condition.
		Comment:	If you/your company reach your/its goals will you/it still be solvent? What must you give up in order to reach the end?
		Reflection:	_____ _____ _____

Coming Out

Station	Direction	Symbol	Description/Reflection
11	Center	Success	Success is that old ABC—ability, breaks and courage. Charles Luckman
		Comment:	What are your abilities? What breaks have you had? Do you have courage? What are the abilities of your company? What breaks has it had or needs to have? What courage does it have?
		Reflection:	_____ _____ _____
12	Bend	Dues	Every advantage has its tax. Ralph Waldo Emerson
		Comment:	What price are you willing to pay for your success? For your company's success? Is the price different? Why?
		Reflection:	_____ _____ _____
13	Bend	Legacy	When we build, let us think that we build forever. John Ruskin
		Comment:	How long do you think the results of your decisions will last? How long do you want them to last? How long is our strategic plan for—1 year, 5 years, 500 years?
		Reflection:	_____ _____ _____
14	Curve	Defeat	There are defeats more triumphant than victories. Montaigne

		Comment:	Can you think about a time you or your company lost and yet it turned out to be a good thing? Why? What did you learn?
		Reflection:	_____ _____ _____
15	Curve	Timing	Our patience will achieve more than our force. Edmund Burke
		Comment:	Does force work in the business world? Why or why not? When have you or your company used it? Has it worked? Why or why not? Is there an alternative? Why have you used it? Why have you not?
		Reflection:	_____ _____ _____
16	Curve	Desperation	It is a characteristic of wisdom not to do desperate things. Thoreau
		Comment:	What does desperation look like? Does your strategic plan have desperation written in it? How can you take it out?
		Reflection:	_____ _____ _____
17	Bend	New Methods	The man who uses yesterday's methods in today's work won't be in business tomorrow.
		Comment:	Does your strategic plan reflect the changes of the global marketplace? Why or why not?
		Reflection:	_____ _____ _____

18	Curve	Belief	A strategy is no good if people don't fundamentally belief in it. Robert Hass
		Comment:	Is the strategic plan communicated throughout the company? Do employees believe it? Why or why not? How can you make them believe?
		Reflection:	_____ _____ _____
19	Bend	Analyze	You can analyze a glass of water and you're left with a lot of chemical components, but nothing you can drink. JBS Haldane
		Comment:	Are you analyzing your company too much? Can you analyze too much? Why analyze at all?
		Reflection:	_____ _____ _____
20	Curve	Finishing	Great is the art of beginning, but greater the art is of ending. Longfellow
		Comment:	Does the strategic plan have an ending? Do you know when you reached your goals?
		Reflection:	_____ _____ _____
21	Out	Finishing	It is not the going out of port, but the coming in, that determines the success of a voyage. Henry Ward Beecher
		Comment:	Where have you arrived and in what condition? How long did it take you to get here? Why?

		Reflection:	

Laberinto #5
Customer Service/Satisfaction

Going In

Station	Direction	Symbol	Description/Reflection
1	In	Delight	It's not enough anymore to merely satisfy the customer. Customers need to be delighted—surprised by having their needs not just met, but excelled. A. Blanton Godfrey
		Comment:	How are you delighting your customers?
		Reflection:	_____ _____ _____
2	Curve	Quality	High quality means pleasing customers not just protecting them from annoyances. David Garvin
		Comment:	What annoyances were you protecting your customers from? Why did those annoyances even exist?
		Reflection:	_____ _____ _____
3	Curve	Loyalty	Real profits are generated by loyal customers—not just satisfied customers. Rafael Aguayo
		Comment:	How can you make your satisfied customers loyal customers? Who are your loyal customers? How do you teat them?
		Reflection:	_____ _____ _____

4	Curve	Perception	It is not enough just to give good services; the customer must perceive that fact that he or she is getting good service. Karl Albrecht and Ron Zemke
		Comment:	Do your customers know what good service they receive from you? Why or why not? How do you know what they think? Do you ask them?
		Reflection:	_____ _____ _____
5	Curve	Statistics	Consumers are statistics. Customers are people. Stanley Marcus
		Comment:	Do you have consumers or customers? How do you let them know that?
		Reflection:	_____ _____ _____
6	Curve	Costs	By far the largest costs that outstanding service saves are those of replacing lost customers. William Davidow and Bro Uttal
		Comment:	How many lost customers have you had in the last 3 years? Why? What can you do to bring them back?
		Reflection:	_____ _____ _____
7	Bend	Expectations	Expectations are what people buy, not things. Theodore Levitt
		Comment:	What do your customers expect? Are you meeting their expectations?
		Reflection:	_____ _____ _____
8	Curve	Listen	The key is to get into the stores and listen. Sam Walton

		Comment:	Do you listen to your customers? How? When? How often? Why?
		Reflection:	_____ _____ _____
9	Bend	Expectations (2)	In the service sector, consumers expect and demand more because they know they can get more. Michael Hammer and James Champy
		Comment:	Why do your customers know they can get more? From you or from who else?
		Reflection:	_____ _____ _____
10	Curve	Guest	In Japanese the same word—oky-akusama—means both "customer" and "honorable guest." Disney World has always thought of its customers as its "guests;" being part of their "family." Customers in today's marketplace are looking for the special treatment that typically honors guests and they are receiving it. Peter Capezio and Debra Morehouse
		Comment:	Are your customers your guests? How can you make them feel so?
		Reflection:	_____ _____ _____
11	Center	Moment of Truth	The moment of truth: any episode in which the customer comes into contact with some aspect of the organization and gets the impression of its service. Karl Albrecht
		Comment:	What has been your moment of truth? How did you fare? How can you make it better?

		Reflection:	

Coming Out

Station	Direction	Symbol	Description/Reflection
11	Center	Discontent	Discontent is the first step in the progress of a man or nation. Oscar Wilde
		Comment:	What are your customers discontented about? How can you change it?
		Reflection:	_____ _____ _____
12	Bend	Experience	Experience is not what happens to a man. It is what man does with what happens to him. Aldous Huxley
		Comment:	What do your customers do with the experience they have with you?
		Reflection:	_____ _____ _____
13	Bend	Luxury	Service. The ultimate luxury. Marriott slogan
		Comment:	Luxury or necessity? How do you view service?
		Reflection:	_____ _____ _____
14	Curve	Fate	We create our fate every day we live. Henry Miller
		Comment:	What does your company do everyday for your customers?
		Reflection:	_____ _____ _____

15	Curve	Chance	A problem is a chance for you to do your best. Duke Ellington
		Comment:	How do you resolve customer problems? How can you do it better?
		Reflection:	_____ _____ _____
16	Curve	Asset	Customers are an economic asset. They are not on the balance sheet but they should be. Prof. Claess Fornell
		Comment:	If they were on your balance sheet how would that change your company's financial value?
		Reflection:	_____ _____ _____
17	Bend	Purpose	The purpose of business is to create and keep a customer. Theodore Levitt
		Comment:	How does your company create a customer? How does it keep it? Can the company improve? How?
		Reflection:	_____ _____ _____
18	Curve	Forget	Never forget a customer. Never let a customer forget you. Frank Bettger
		Comment:	How are you memorable to your customers?
		Reflection:	_____ _____ _____
19	Bend	Overdeliver	When it comes to customer service underpromise and overdeliver. Paul R. Timm

		Comment:	What do you overpromise and underdeliver? How can you change this?
		Reflection:	
20	Curve	Finding Faults	The fault-finder will find faults even in paradise. Henry David Thoreau
		Comment:	What are you nick-picking at? Focus on the big things that affect your customers. What are they?
		Reflection:	
21	Out	Sense of Humor	A keen sense of humor helps us to overlook the unbecoming, understand the unconventional, tolerate the unpleasant, overcome the unexpected, and outlast the unbearable. Billy Graham
		Comment:	Does your company have a sense of humor aligned with that of your customers? Do your employees smile?
		Reflection:	

Laberinto #6
Marketing

Going In

Station	Direction	Symbol	Description/Reflection
1	In	Unknown	No one desires what is unknown. Ovid
		Comment:	What does the world know about you, your company, your product or your service? If you don't know what they know how can you find out?
		Reflection:	_____ _____ _____
2	Curve	Advertising	The advertisements in a newspaper are more full of knowledge in respect to what is going on in a state or community than the editorial columns are. Henry Ward Beecher
		Comment:	Does your marketing reflect what is happening today in society? Can your customers relate to it?
		Reflection:	_____ _____ _____
3	Curve	Promise	Promise, large promise, is the soul of an advertisement. Samuel Johnson
		Comment:	What promises are you making in your marketing campaign? Are they empty promises or can your company fulfill them?
		Reflection:	_____ _____ _____

4	Curve	Substitutes	Ours is the age of substitutes; instead of language we have jargon; instead of principles, slogans; and instead of genuine ideas, bright ideas. Eric Bentley
		Comment:	What substitutes exists for your products and services? What substitutes exist for your company? What substitute exists for you?
		Reflection:	_____ _____ _____
5	Curve	Uses	Sweet are the uses of advertisement.
		Comment:	What do you use advertising for? Is it for the right reasons? Can something else fulfill that need instead of advertising?
		Reflection:	_____ _____ _____
6	Curve	Press	The hand that rules the press rules the country. Learned Hand
		Comment:	What kind of relationships does your company have with the media? Do you know your local, state, regional, national and international media? How can you get to know them so they can get to know you and your company?
		Reflection:	_____ _____ _____
7	Bend	Statistics	Statistics can be made to prove anything—even the truth.
		Comment:	What does your marketing campaign use statistics for? What do they prove? What do you need them to prove?

		Reflection:	
8	Curve	Advertising (2)	Advertising nourishes the consuming power of man…it spurs individual exertion and greater production. Sir Winston Churchill
		Comment:	Does advertising have a role in the greater good of society? What is that role? Why can only advertising fulfill it?
		Reflection:	
9	Bend	Jingle	A very great part of the pleasure people take in music comes from the association it revives. Leland Hall
		Comment:	Does your marketing campaign have a jingle—some music that serves to identify your company? Is it beautiful music or background noise? Is it effective? What does it make the customer relate to?
		Reflection:	
10	Curve	Society	Society is, in general, profoundly indifferent and forgetful. Andre Maurois
		Comment:	How can you make society not forget you or your company? How can you make your customers care?
		Reflection:	
11	Center	Craft	Advertising is a craft and it has to be learned. It is not something that consumers can do successfully. Ellis Verdi

		Comment:	Do you have professionals doing your marketing? Are they effective? If you do it yourself, are you effective? Why or why not? What would make it more effective?
		Reflection:	_____ _____ _____

Coming Out

Station	Direction	Symbol	Description/Reflection
11	Center	Ego	Ego is a treacherous and debilitating force. Nowhere is that more true than in marketing and product design. Arnold Hiatt
		Comment:	Is your marketing and product design effective in communicating to your customers or is it full of self-references and self-indulgences?
		Reflection:	_____ _____ _____
12	Bend	Words	It is astonishing what power words have over man. Napoleon Bonaparte
		Comment:	What is your slogan? What is the catch phrase for your marketing campaign? Is it powerful enough? Does it work? Do your customers understand it? Why or why not? If they don't how can you change it?
		Reflection:	_____ _____ _____
13	Bend	Big Idea	Unless your campaign has a big idea it will pass like a ship in the night. David Ogilvy
		Comment:	What is your campaign's big idea? Why is it a big idea? Is it a big idea only to your company or also to your customers?
		Reflection:	_____ _____ _____
14	Curve	Identity	Good packages create companies. Elinor Selane

		Comment:	How do you package your products and/or services? How do you package your company? Your employees? Do your customers recognize the packaging as uniquely yours? Why or why not?
		Reflection:	_____ _____ _____
15	Curve	Brand	To make a brand persuasive in the consumer's mind you need to use all the channels of communication, not just television. Ken Robbins
		Comment:	What channels of communication do you use for your marketing? Are you limiting yourself? Where could you market if you had very little money? Try something different and creative.
		Reflection:	_____ _____ _____
16	Curve	Global	Even underwear has national characteristics. John Bryon, Hanes
		Comment:	Are you doing international marketing? Is it working? Why or why not? Do you respect the other culture in your marketing? Do you even know the other culture? What can you do to learn it?
		Reflection:	_____ _____ _____
17	Bend	Demographics	We become slaves to demographics, to market research, to focus groups. We produce what the numbers tell us to produce. And gradually, in this dizzying chase, our senses lose feeling and our instincts dim, corroded with safe action. Barry Diller

		Comment:	Why do you produce what you produce?
		Reflection:	_____
18	Curve	Words (2)	Words calculated to catch everyone may catch no one. Adlai E. Stevenson Jr.
		Comment:	Who is your target audience? Is your marketing effective in reaching them? Why or why not?
		Reflection:	_____
19	Bend	Interviews	It's always dangerous to give interviews. Steve Jobs
		Comment:	What do you say to the press? Are you consistent every time they reach out to you? Do you remember what you told them last time?
		Reflection:	_____
20	Curve	Color	Why is a carrot more orange than an orange? Amboy Duke
		Comment:	Are you portraying yourself as an original or as a better-than-the-original in your marketing? Why?
		Reflection:	_____
21	Out	Worth	Everything is worth what its purchaser will pay for it. Publius Syrus
		Comment:	What is your company, product, service worth to your customers? Does your marketing reflect this?

		Reflection:	

Laberinto #7
Creativity and Innovation

Going In

Station	Direction	Symbol	Description/Reflection
1	In	See	It is not what you look at that matters, it's what you see. Henry David Thoreau
		Comment:	What do you see when you look at your company? Your products? Your services? Do you see "what is" or "what can be?"
		Reflection:	_____ _____ _____
2	Curve	Set Free	I saw an angel in the marble and carved until I set him free. Michelangelo Buonarroti
		Comment:	What can you set free in your company?
		Reflection:	_____ _____ _____
3	Curve	Unknown	Creativity requires the courage to let go of certainties. Erich Fromm
		Comment:	What certainty can you/your company let go of? How will this bring you to the next level?
		Reflection:	_____ _____ _____
4	Curve	Difficulty	The difficult is what takes a little time; the impossible is what takes a little longer. Fridtjof Nansen

		Comment:	Think of something impossible in relation to your job/company. How can you make it happen?
		Reflection:	_____ _____ _____
5	Curve	Connection	When one tugs at a single thing in nature, he finds it attached to the rest of the world. John Muir
		Comment:	One creative thought will lead to another. How do they connect? Look at the connections? How can you use the connections for success?
		Reflection:	_____ _____ _____
6	Curve	Perspective	Discovery consists of seeing what everyone has seen and thinking what no one has thought. Albert von Szent-gyorgyi
		Comment:	What is the current trend? How can you modify it to provide something unique?
		Reflection:	_____ _____ _____
7	Bend	Kernel	The creation of a thousand forests is in one acorn. Ralph Waldo Emerson
		Comment:	What little ideas are brewing in your company? How can these ideas grow? What do they need? How can you nourish them? Who has these ideas? How can you nourish the idea makers?

		Reflection:	_____ _____ _____
8	Curve	Art	Art is either plagiarism or revolution. Paul Ganguin
		Comment:	Everything begins from something else—remember the connections above? How would your product or service revolutionize your customers?
		Reflection:	_____ _____ _____
9	Bend	Break Rules	There is no rule that may not be broken in the pursuit of a greater beauty. Ludwig van Beethoven
		Comment:	How can you break with tradition without it being revolutionary?
		Reflection:	_____ _____ _____
10	Curve	Birth	The business of every art is to bring something into existence. Aristotle
		Comment:	What does your company bring into existence? Is it needed by your customers? By society? By you?
		Reflection:	_____ _____ _____
11	Center	Danger	All great ideas are dangerous. Oscar Wilde
		Comment:	What great and dangerous ideas do you have? How can you make it reality? Why would you want to? Or why not?

		Reflection:	
			_____ _____ _____

Coming Out

Station	Direction	Symbol	Description/Reflection
11	Center	Cultivate	We must cultivate our garden. Voltaire
		Comment:	What is your garden or your company's garden? What do you grow? How do you nourish it?
		Reflection:	_____ _____ _____
12	Bend	Curiosity	Curiosity is one of the permanent and certain characteristics of a vigorous intellect. Samuel Johnson
		Comment:	What are you curious about? Think of three questions you would like answers to. Research them. What did you learn?
		Reflection:	_____ _____ _____
13	Bend	Solving Problems	Creativity can solve almost any problem. The creative act, the defeat of habit by originality, overcomes everything. George Lois
		Comment:	What can you do differently from your everyday routine? Try it. What happened?
		Reflection:	_____ _____ _____
14	Curve	Science	Men love to wonder and that is the seed of our science. Ralph Waldo Emerson
		Comment:	What do you wonder about? What do your customers wonder about?

		Reflection:	_____ _____ _____
15	Curve	Advantage	Many men are successful because they didn't have the advantages other men had.
		Comment:	How did you overcome your disadvantages? How can you use that experience now?
		Reflection:	_____ _____ _____
16	Curve	Borrow	I not only have use of all the brains I have, but all I can borrow. Woodrow Wilson
		Comment:	Who do your surround yourself with? What do your contacts know? How do you network? How often do you network? Are you an effective networker? Why or why not? How can you learn to be more effective?
		Reflection:	_____ _____ _____
17	Bend	Gray	The enemy of all painting is the color gray. Delacroix
		Comment:	What colors do you paint your world in? Why?
		Reflection:	_____ _____ _____
18	Curve	Manage	The great requisite for the prosperous management of ordinary business is the want of imagination. Hazlitt
		Comment:	How do you use your imagination? Why? Can you use it more often? How?

		Reflection:	_____ _____ _____
19	Bend	Travel	Travel develops a man's mind especially his imagination.
		Comment:	How often do you travel? Does not have to be overseas, it could be down the block or through a book. How can you travel more? What do you do when you travel? Why?
		Reflection:	_____ _____ _____
20	Curve	The Unthinkable	Creativity requires the freedom to consider "unthinkable" alternatives, to doubt the worth of cherished practices. John W. Gardner
		Comment:	What is unthinkable to you or your company? Why?
		Reflection:	_____ _____ _____
21	Out	Innovation	Knowledge applied to existing processes, services and products is productivity; knowledge applied to the new is innovation. Peter Drucker
		Comment:	How do you or your company innovate? Is it enough?
		Reflection:	_____ _____ _____

Laberinto #8
Leadership

Going In

Station	Direction	Symbol	Description/Reflection
1	In	Need	People need a leader. Steven Caps (Apple)
		Comment:	Who is a leader in your company? Are you one? Why or why not? Who is your leader?
		Reflection:	_____ _____ _____
2	Curve	Reality	The first responsibility of a leader is to define reality. Max de Pree
		Comment:	What is your company's reality? How is it defined by your company's leader?
		Reflection:	_____ _____ _____
3	Curve	Belief in Mission	If we fight with faith we are twice armed. Plato
		Comment:	Do you believe your leader? If you are the leader, do your followers believe in you? Enough to fight?
		Reflection:	_____ _____ _____
4	Curve	Careful	It is from care that blessings arise. It is from carelessness that troubles arise. Buddha
		Comment:	Does your leader care? How does he/she show it? As a leader how do you show you care? Why is it important that followers know you care?

		Reflection:	
5	Curve	Wisdom	Power without wisdom collapses under its own weight. Horace
		Comment:	Is your leader wise or is she/he only powerful? Are you wise or only powerful? What makes you wise? How can you become wise?
		Reflection:	
6	Curve	Priorities	Besides the noble art of getting things done, there is the noble art of leaving things undone. The wisdom of life consists in the elimination of non-essentials. Lin Yutang
		Comment:	What are you doing that you can delegate to another or not have done at all?
		Reflection:	
7	Bend	Focus	The sun, with all those planets revolving around it and depending on it, can still ripen a bunch of grapes as if it had nothing else in the universe to do. Galileo Galilei
		Comment:	Are you always rushing to get things done or do you take your time? Do followers feel they got all your attention for their important matter or do they feel brushed off?
		Reflection:	
8	Curve	Equality	A feeling of superiority is a sign of failure. Yoshida Kenko

		Comment:	Do you feel superior to others? Does your leader make you feel inferior? Why?
		Reflection:	_____ _____ _____
9	Bend	Anarchy	Anarchy is the stepping stone to absolute power. Napoleon Bonaparte
		Comment:	How does your leader make decisions? As a leader how do you make decisions?
		Reflection:	_____ _____ _____
10	Curve	King	The king is the man who can. Thomas Carlyle
		Comment:	What can your leader do? What can you as a leader do?
		Reflection:	_____ _____ _____
11	Center	Self-Control	How shall I be able to rule over others if I have not full power and command of myself? François Rabelais
		Comment:	Does your leader lose his/her temper? Do you as a leader lose your temper? Your cool? How can you maintain calm?
		Reflection:	_____ _____ _____

Coming Out

Station	Direction	Symbol	Description/Reflection
11	Center	Self	You must be the change you wish to see in the world. Mahatma Gandhi
		Comment:	What change do you want to see in the world? In your company? How can you make it happen?
		Reflection:	_____ _____ _____
12	Bend	Enemy	Authority is never without hate. Euripides
		Comment:	Why do leaders have enemies? As a leader do you have those who hate you/dislike you? Why? Can you change their perception of you or should you leave it alone? Why?
		Reflection:	_____ _____ _____
13	Bend	Learn from Others	The reading of all good books is like conversation with the finest men of past centuries. Rene Descartes
		Comment:	Queen Elizabeth I of England spent 4 hours a day reading history. She is acknowledged as one of the greatest leaders of all time. What do you read? What do your leaders read?
		Reflection:	_____ _____ _____
14	Curve	Greatness	'Tis the men, not the houses that make the city. Thomas Fuller

		Comment:	How do followers make a leader? How did you become a leader? How can you unite your followers to make a cohesive whole (whether a company or a team)?
		Reflection:	_____ _____ _____
15	Curve	Decision	Nothing is more difficulty and therefore more precious, then to be able to decide. Napoleon Bonaparte
		Comment:	Do your leaders make decisions or do they never get around to it? As a leader do you make decisions—how do you make them?
		Reflection:	_____ _____ _____
16	Curve	Deeds	Men are all alike in their promises. It is only in their deeds that they differ. Moliere
		Comment:	What deeds make your leaders stand out? What deeds make you as a leader stand out?
		Reflection:	_____ _____ _____
17	Bend	Difficult Times	Any one can hold the helm when the sea is calm. Publius Syrus
		Comment:	What kind of leader do you need in a crisis? Are you that kind? Why or why not? Can you become that kind?
		Reflection:	_____ _____ _____
18	Curve	Focus	Lost in the solitude of his immense power, he began to lose direction. Gabriel Garcia Marques

		Comment:	Does your leader still have focus or has power gone to his head? As a leader, do you still have focus or has power gone to your head?
		Reflection:	_____ _____ _____
19	Bend	Power	The property of power is to protect. Pascal
		Comment:	Does your leader protect you? Your company? As a leader do you protect your followers? Your employees? Your company?
		Reflection:	_____ _____ _____
20	Curve	Action	What you do speaks so loud that I cannot hear what you say. Ralph Waldo Emerson
		Comment:	Do you do what you say you will do? Do your leaders do what they say they will do? If not, why are they still your leader?
		Reflection:	_____ _____ _____
21	Out	Glorious	How glorious it is—and also how painful—to be an exception. Alfred de Musset
		Comment:	As a leader are you alone? Why? Do you accept the position?
		Reflection:	_____ _____ _____

Laberinto #9
Negotiation

Going In

Station	Direction	Symbol	Description/Reflection
1	In	Fear	Let us never negotiate out of fear, but let us never fear to negotiate. John F. Kennedy
		Comment:	The first step in negotiation is to decide to negotiate. What is holding you back from negotiating? How can you resolve your objections?
		Reflection:	_____ _____ _____
2	Curve	Agreement	Agreement is brought about by changing people's minds—other peoples. S. I. Hayakawa
		Comment:	Would you allow someone to change your mind? Why do you expect to change someone else's mind then? We can only change our own mind. How can we help them change their own mind? How can they help us change our own mind?
		Reflection:	_____ _____ _____
3	Curve	Principle	When diplomats say they agree in principle, it means they agree in nothing else.
		Comment:	What do both parties agree on? Why? Start with that.
		Reflection:	_____ _____ _____

4	Curve	Quiet	A good way to get people to agree with you is to keep your mouth shut.
		Comment:	There are some things that should not be said. Think back to a time you said something you shouldn't have? How can you prevent that from happening?
		Reflection:	_____ _____ _____
5	Curve	Convince	The less sound a man's argument, the louder he talks.
		Comment:	How aggravated is the other party getting? Why? Maintain your cool. How can you help them become calm?
		Reflection:	_____ _____ _____
6	Curve	Boil	We boil at different degrees. Ralph Waldo Emerson
		Comment:	Do you know your limit? Do you know the other side's limit? Do not push it past the limit.
		Reflection:	_____ _____ _____
7	Bend	What to Say	A diplomat always knows what to talk about but doesn't always talk about what he knows.
		Comment:	Do you know what to say and when to say it? Think of a time you said the right thing at the right time. How did you feel? Can you repeat that?
		Reflection:	_____ _____ _____

8	Curve	Writing	Writing things down is the best secret of a good memory.
		Comment:	Do you take notes when you are negotiating? How do you know what you negotiated if you didn't take notes? Did the other party take notes? Compare your notes. Are you on the same page?
		Reflection:	_____
9	Bend	Tiresome	The man who only knows one subject is almost as tiresome as the man who knows no subject. Charles Dickens
		Comment:	When you negotiate do you only know that deal or do you know of other deals and how they were solved? Are you narrowly focused or open to alternatives?
		Reflection:	_____
10	Curve	Whisper	What I like in a good author is not what he says but what he whispers. Logan P. Smith
		Comment:	What are the undertones in a negotiation? What is the body language telling you? What are the nonverbal signs the other party is throwing out? What nonverbal signs are you throwing out?
		Reflection:	_____
11	Center	Willingness	In business, willingness is just as important as ability—Paul G. Hoffman
		Comment:	What are you willing to do to have a successful negotiation? Why?

		Reflection:	

Coming Out

Station	Direction	Symbol	Description/Reflection
11	Center	Establish	Decide what you want, decide what you are willing to exchange for it. Establish your priorities and go to work. H. L. Hunt
		Comment:	Are you prepared when you go into a negotiation? Why or why not? How can you prepare better?
		Reflection:	_____ _____ _____
12	Bend	Tired	Tired people make bad decisions. That's something Ronald Reagan told me. Dick Jenrette, CEO, Equitable
		Comment:	Do you take breaks when you negotiate or do you struggle through the fatigue and hunger? What kind of agreement do you end up with in each case?
		Reflection:	_____ _____ _____
13	Bend	Commerce	Commerce is the greatest of all political interests. Joseph Chamberlain
		Comment:	What interests are there when you negotiate? Do you want to continue commerce with the other party or do you want to terminate all ties? The answer to this question will determine how you proceed.
		Reflection:	_____ _____ _____

14	Curve	Reason	A man always has two reasons for what he does—a good one and the real one. JP Morgan
		Comment:	Know your reasons for negotiating and for why you agree or disagree with a term. Can a good reason be the same as a real one? Why or why not? Are they mutually exclusive? Why or why not?
		Reflection:	_____ _____ _____
15	Curve	Promote Your Cause	You don't promote the cause of peace by talking only to people with whom you agree. Dwight Eisenhower
		Comment:	Do you listen to people who make statements you don't agree with? Why or why not? Should you? Why or why not? How does this play out in a negotiation?
		Reflection:	_____ _____ _____
16	Curve	Imagination	Imagination is more important than knowledge. Albert Einstein
		Comment:	How can imagination help you in a negotiation?
		Reflection:	_____ _____ _____
17	Bend	Perception	It is the commonest of mistakes to consider that the limit of our power of perception is also the limit of all there is to perceive. CW Leadbeater
		Comment:	What are you not allowing yourself to see in the negotiation? How can you take your blinders off?

		Reflection:	
18	Curve	Responsibility	The price of greatness is responsibility. Winston Churchill
		Comment:	Are you ready to assume the responsibility for the agreement of the negotiation? Why or why not?
		Reflection:	
19	Bend	What Matters	Things that matter most must never be at the mercy of things which matter least. Goethe
		Comment:	What are you sacrificing to reach an agreement? Is it worth it? What are your priorities?
		Reflection:	
20	Curve	Deserve	In business you don't get what you deserve, you get what you negotiate. Chester L. Karrass
		Comment:	What do you negotiate for? What should you negotiate for? Why do you not negotiate for it?
		Reflection:	
21	Out	Finished	As Yogi Berra says "it's not over till it's over" and that's true of negotiations as well. Owen Bieber
		Comment:	When do you know the negotiation is over? How do you leave the table? The room? How will this affect future negotiations?

		Reflection:	
			_____
			_____
			_____

Laberinto #10
Business Wisdom (2)

Going In

Station	Direction	Symbol	Description/Reflection
1	In	Presence	80% of success is showing up. Woody Allen
		Comment:	Are you present in your job? In your company? In your life?
		Reflection:	_____ _____ _____
2	Curve	Law	Laws are not invented, they grow out of circumstances. Azarias
		Comment:	What rules and policies are required in your company? Why? Is there anything you can do to make them unnecessary?
		Reflection:	_____ _____ _____
3	Curve	Time	Next week there can't be any crisis. My schedule is full. Henry A. Kissinger
		Comment:	Can you schedule when crisis will hit? How can you better prepare yourself to deal with them then?
		Reflection:	_____ _____ _____
4	Curve	Facts	Facts do not cease to exist because they are ignored. Aldous Huxley

		Comment:	What facts are you ignoring to your own peril? Why are you ignoring them?
		Reflection:	_____ _____ _____
5	Curve	Belief	People readily believe what they want to believe. Julius Cesar
		Comment:	What do you believe because you want to believe it? What about the employees in the company?
		Reflection:	_____ _____ _____
6	Curve	Invisible	I am invisible…simple because people refuse to see me. Ralph Ellison
		Comment:	Who do you refuse to see in your company? Who refuses to see you? How can you open their eyes?
		Reflection:	_____ _____ _____
7	Bend	Crisis	When written in Chinese the word "crisis" is composed of two characters—one represents "danger" and the other represents "opportunity." John F. Kennedy
		Comment:	What opportunities came out of a recent crisis you had to deal with? What did you learn?
		Reflection:	_____ _____ _____
8	Curve	Deeds	Our deeds determine us as much as we determine our deeds. George Eliot

		Comment:	How do you select what tasks or projects you will work on? What is the criteria? Why do you use these criteria? Where did you get them from?
		Reflection:	_____ _____ _____
9	Bend	Duty	You will always find those who think they know what your duty is better than you know it. Ralph Waldo Emerson
		Comment:	Who is looking to replace you? Why do they think they can do a better job than you? Who do you want to replace? Why do you think you can do a better job then them?
		Reflection:	_____ _____ _____
10	Curve	Human Nature	Knowledge of human nature is the beginning and the end of political education. Henry Adams
		Comment:	How well a judge of character are you? Why?
		Reflection:	_____ _____ _____
11	Center	The Moment	Any life, no matter how long and complex it may be, is made up of a single moment—the moment in which a man finds out, once and for all, who he is. Jorge Luis Borges
		Comment:	When did you find out who you are?
		Reflection:	_____ _____ _____

Coming Out

Station	Direction	Symbol	Description/Reflection
11	Center	Growth	Growth is the only evidence of life. John Henry Newman
		Comment:	How are you growing?
		Reflection:	_____ _____ _____
12	Bend	Attempt	Nothing will ever be attempted if all possible objections must first be overcome. Samuel Johnson
		Comment:	What objections are keeping you from pursuing a new challenge or new project?
		Reflection:	_____ _____ _____
13	Bend	Experience	Experience is a hard teacher because she gives the test first, the lesson after. Vernon Law
		Comment:	Think about a recent experience that taught you a hard lesson.
		Reflection:	_____ _____ _____
14	Curve	Genius	Men of genius are meteors, destined to burn themselves out in lighting up their age. Napoleon Bonaparte
		Comment:	What are you burning up doing? Can you still achieve your goal without burning up?
		Reflection:	_____ _____ _____

15	Curve	Leadership	There are men who, by their sympathetic attractions carry nations with them. Ralph Waldo Emerson
		Comment:	Are you willing to carry your company with you on your decisions?
		Reflection:	_____
16	Curve	Ambition	A slave has just one master; an ambitious person has as many masters as there are people useful to him. La Bruyere
		Comment:	How many masters do you have? Who are they? Why are they your masters?
		Reflection:	_____
17	Bend	Wisdom	The beginning of wisdom is to call things by their right names. Chinese Proverb
		Comment:	Do you know their names? Those of your team members, employees, customers, family?
		Reflection:	_____
18	Curve	Wit	Wit is the salt of conversation. William Hazlitt
		Comment:	Are you tactful in your conversations?
		Reflection:	_____
19	Bend	Purpose	Companies exist in a society for the purpose of satisfying people in that society. Ishikawa

		Comment:	Why does your company exist? Why do you exist in your company?
		Reflection:	_____ _____ _____
20	Curve	Definition	Companies can be thought of as bundles of skills, capabilities and competencies. Robert Waterman
		Comment:	Can you identify the skills, capabilities and competences of your company? Of yourself?
		Reflection:	_____ _____ _____
21	Out	Prepared	Chance favors only the mind that is prepared. Louis Pasteur
		Comment:	Are you prepared? How can you make yourself more prepared?
		Reflection:	_____ _____ _____

Laberinto #11
International Business

Going In

Station	Direction	Symbol	Description/Reflection
1	In	Travel	There is an inexhaustible source of wisdom. Alfred Lord Tennyson
		Comment:	Do you know where to go to get the answers you need before you venture into international waters?
		Reflection:	_____
2	Curve	Home	A wise traveler never despises his own country. William Hazlitt
		Comment:	Do you continue to do business in your home country or have you given it up to look overseas?
		Reflection:	_____
3	Curve	Location	He that is everywhere is nowhere. Thomas Fuller
		Comment:	Have you spread yourself out too thin in too many different countries at once?
		Reflection:	_____
4	Curve	Difference	Japanese and American management is 95% the same and different in all important matters. Takeo Fugisana (Honda)
		Comment:	What is that other 5% made up of? How can you find out?

		Reflection:	_____ _____ _____
5	Curve	Overcoming Obstacles	I believe in the power of great art to transcend geographical boundaries, political differences and even the restrictions of time. Armand Hammer
		Comment:	How does the art and culture of one country influence another's? How is your company involved in this inter-change?
		Reflection:	_____ _____ _____
6	Curve	Books	Books are the treasured wealth of the world and the fit inheritance of genera-tions and nations. David Thoreau
		Comment:	What books do you have about other cultures and counties of the world? Do you read them? Why or why not? What can you learn to help you become a success?
		Reflection:	_____ _____ _____
7	Bend	Partners	An agreeable companion on a journey is as good as a carriage. Publilius Syrus
		Comment:	Who are your international partners? How did you select them? Why?
		Reflection:	_____ _____ _____
8	Curve	Custom	Custom is the guide of the ignorant. English Proverb

		Comment:	Observe what is happening in the country you plan to do business in. What did you learn that will affect your success?
		Reflection:	
9	Bend	Size	Size is not grandeur and territory does not make a nation. Thomas Henry Huxley
		Comment:	Culture transcends boundaries. Where is the new country located? Where are its citizens located?
		Reflection:	
10	Curve	Idea	An idea does not pass from one language to another without change. Miguel de Unamuno
		Comment:	Who does your translations? Do you know more than one language? Can you translate? What gets lost in translation? How can you get it back?
		Reflection:	
11	Center	Morality	Money, not morality, is the principle of commerce and commercial nations. Thomas Jefferson
		Comment:	Is money the only thing? What are you looking for?
		Reflection:	

Coming Out

Station	Direction	Symbol	Description/Reflection
11	Center	Being Global	Being global is not just where you do business but how you do business. Stephen D. Harlan, KPMG
		Comment:	What does your company do that proves it is an international company?
		Reflection:	_____ _____ _____
12	Bend	Accent	Man is the only animal to whom accent is important.
		Comment:	Why do we care where people are from? Why do we care if someone has an accent?
		Reflection:	_____ _____ _____
13	Bend	Advancement	The process of advancement is interesting; it isn't that you get bigger to fit the world; the world gets smaller to fit you. TS Eliot
		Comment:	How does the world get smaller?
		Reflection:	_____ _____ _____
14	Curve	Steps	The first step binds one to the second. French Proverb
		Comment:	What did you start and have to finish? Why did you start it?
		Reflection:	_____ _____ _____

15	Curve	Hiring	Diversity isn't a slogan—it's a reality when you're hiring people everywhere. Robert M. Teeter, UPS Board Member
		Comment:	How diverse is your staff? Your customer base? Your family?
		Reflection:	_____
16	Curve	Law	Be in countries where there is a good legal system and a respect for property rights. Charles Target
		Comment:	Are you familiar with the legal systems of the countries your company does business in? how do these laws protect the company? How do these laws leave you susceptible to liability?
		Reflection:	_____
17	Bend	Technology	Technology travels with people. Chuck Geschke, Adobe Systems
		Comment:	When your company does business overseas what technology does it use? Does it leave the technology there? What technology does it bring back?
		Reflection:	_____
18	Curve	Market	A Mercedes has enormous cachet in Britain, but in Germany, it's a taxi. Donal Gunn
		Comment:	What is the value of your products and/or services in the different countries you do business in? What accounts for the differences?

		Reflection:	_____ _____ _____
19	Bend	Business Plan	Columbus didn't have a business plan when he discovered America. Andrew Grove, Intel
		Comment:	But he died never knowing where he was! (He thought he had reached India). Do you know where you are?
		Reflection:	_____ _____ _____
20	Curve	Prosperity	Nothings contribute as much to the prosperity and happiness of a country as high profits. David Ricardo
		Comment:	What high profits are you bringing to your home country and to the countries you do business in? Do you bring or get anything other than profits? What is more important?
		Reflection:	_____ _____ _____
21	Out	Knowledge	The knowledge of the world is only to be acquired in the world and not in a closet. Lord Chesterfield
		Comment:	Have you traveled to the countries your company does business in? Why or why not?
		Reflection:	_____ _____ _____

Laberinto #12
Technology

Going In

Station	Direction	Symbol	Description/Reflection
1	In	Miracle	The miraculousness of technology is a popular article of Western faith. Michael Harrington
		Comment:	Why do you believe in technology? What do you believe technology can accomplish or do for you? For your company? For society?
		Reflection:	_____ _____ _____
2	Curve	Technology	Technology feeds itself. Technology makes more technology possible. Alvin Toffler
		Comment:	With what technology did your company start with? How much technology does your company have now? Does it help?
		Reflection:	_____ _____ _____
3	Curve	Global Nerve	Is it a fact—or have I dreamed it—that by means of electricity the world of matter has become a great nerve, vibrating thousands of miles in a breathless point of time? Nathaniel Hawthorne
		Comment:	This was stated in 1851. How does this nerve look now?
		Reflection:	_____ _____ _____

4	Curve	Man	Man is still the most extraordinary computer of all. John F. Kennedy
		Comment:	Man created the computer. Does it make us superior to it? Are we superior to technology? How? Why?
		Reflection:	_____ _____ _____
5	Curve	Knowledge	Knowledge is getting to be more and more costly, with most of the cost required in classifying it.
		Comment:	How much is information gathering, formatting, analyzing and distributing costing your company? Costing you in terms of time, etc.? How can you lower the costs?
		Reflection:	_____ _____ _____
6	Curve	Automation	If automation is so efficient, why doesn't it replace the ladder of success with an escalator?
		Comment:	Some things cannot be automated. Can you think of some examples?
		Reflection:	_____ _____ _____
7	Bend	Progress	Progress always means change, but change doesn't always mean progress.
		Comment:	How do you define change? How do you define progress? How does your company define progress?
		Reflection:	_____ _____ _____

8	Curve	Weakest Link	The weakest link in a chain is its strongest because it can break it. Stanislan J. Lee
		Comment:	What is your company's weakest and strongest link? What kind of security system does it have?
		Reflection:	_____ _____ _____
9	Bend	Faith	When there is the necessary technical skill to move mountains, there is no need for the faith that moves mountains. Eric Hoffer
		Comment:	Why do we need to move mountains at all?
		Reflection:	_____ _____ _____
10	Curve	Progress (2)	Problems are the prize you pay for progress. Branch Rickey
		Comment:	Is that a good thing?
		Reflection:	_____ _____ _____
11	Center	Real Problems	The real problem is not whether machines think but whether men do. BF Skinner
		Comment:	Do you think? Are there things that you let your computer think for you? Are you too dependent on technology?
		Reflection:	_____ _____ _____

Coming Out

Station	Direction	Symbol	Description/Reflection
11	Center	Magic	Any sufficiently advanced technology is indistinguishable from magic. Arthur C Clarke
		Comment:	What is the magic? What technology do you still see as magic? Why?
		Reflection:	_____ _____ _____
12	Bend	Strategy	Strategy is easy, implementation is hard. Raymond Smith, Bell Atlantic
		Comment:	Technology looks promising in the brochure. How does it look in your company?
		Reflection:	_____ _____ _____
13	Bend	Internet	If someone thinks they are being mistreated by us they won't tell 5 people—they'll tell 5,000. Jeffrey Bezos, Amazon
		Comment:	Do your customers and employees have access to the Internet? Do they use it to counter-market against you?
		Reflection:	_____ _____ _____
14	Curve	Savior	Technology is not the savior; it is the enabler. All too often organizations start with technology and then do not achieve the business objective. James A Unruh, CEO, Unisys

		Comment:	Does the technology in your company serve the company's ultimate goals? Why or why not?
		Reflection:	_____
15	Curve	CEOs/PCs	There are CEOs who brag about never having touched a PC. I say to them "get your head out of the sand kid." Charles Wang
		Comment:	Do you use computers in your daily work or do you delegate that to someone else? Do you use email? Do you answer your own? Why or why not?
		Reflection:	_____
16	Curve	Security	Any system is subject to someone getting around it. Michael Carpenter, CEO, Kidder Peabody
		Comment:	Has anyone ever infiltrated your network system? How did they do it? Has the security been updated? Do you change passwords? Eliminate terminated employees passwords?
		Reflection:	_____
17	Bend	Concern	Concern for man and his fate must always form the chief interest of all technical endeavors. Never forget this in the midst of your diagrams and equations. Albert Einstein
		Comment:	Does you company concern itself with its employees when it adopts new technology?

		Reflection:	
18	Curve	GIGO	Garbage in, garbage out. Anonymous
		Comment:	How do you apply quality control for the information in your company databases?
		Reflection:	
19	Bend	Building Blocks	The three building blocks of business are hardware, software and "humanware." Masaaki Imai
		Comment:	How does your company's humanware interact with the hardware and software?
		Reflection:	
20	Curve	Question	Technology is the answer—now what was the question? R. Paul
		Comment:	What questions are you trying to answer with technology at your company?
		Reflection:	
21	Out	Computers/ Future	Computers are magnificent tools for the realization of our dreams, but no machine can replace the human spark of spirit, compassion, love and understanding. Louis Gersten, CEO, IBM

| | | *Comment:* | Are you using technology to replace the irreplaceable? Is your company attempting this? Why? Should it continue? Why or why not? |
| | | *Reflection:* | _____ |

Laberinto #13
Communication

Going In

Station	Direction	Symbol	Description/Reflection
1	In	Language	The limits of my language are the limits of my world. Ludwig Wittgenstein
		Comment:	Do you continue to increase your vocabulary skills? Why or why not?
		Reflection:	_____ _____ _____
2	Curve	Principle	I detest what you write, but I would give my life to make it possible for you to continue to write. Voltaire
		Comment:	Freedom of speech is a right protected by the First Amendment. How do you express this right? What do you write about and why? Where have you gotten published? Have you tried to get published? Why or why not?
		Reflection:	_____ _____ _____
3	Curve	Argument	Arguments only confirm people in their own opinions. Booth Tarkington
		Comment:	When you communicate your argument are you convincing the other party or yourself?
		Reflection:	_____ _____ _____
4	Curve	Memos	A memorandum is written not to inform the reader but to protect the writer. Wall street Journal

		Comment:	When do you write a memo? What do you write memos about? Do you store them? Why?
		Reflection:	_____ _____ _____
5	Curve	Change	Language does not stand still, surprisingly despite this knowledge, most speakers are fearful of change. Peter Farb
		Comment:	Do you change your expressions? Your words? Your thoughts? Why or why not?
		Reflection:	_____ _____ _____
6	Curve	Express	Much unhappiness has come into the world because of bewilderment and things left unsaid. Dostoyevsky
		Comment:	What needs to be said that you are not saying? To whom?
		Reflection:	_____ _____ _____
7	Bend	Secrets	To whom you tell your secrets, to him you resign your liberty. Spanish Proverb
		Comment:	Who is your confidante? Why do you trust this person? Who else knows your secrets? Can you trust them? Why or why not? If not, why do they know your secrets? Why do you have secrets anyway?
		Reflection:	_____ _____ _____

8	Curve	Dialogue	A conversation is a dialogue, not a monologue. Truman Capote
		Comment:	Are you in a dialogue or a monologue? Is the person you are conversing with in a dialogue or a monologue? How do you know?
		Reflection:	_____ _____ _____
9	Bend	Listening	The art of conversation is the art of hearing as well as of being heard. William Hazlitt
		Comment:	How are your listening skills? Test them out. What did you learn?
		Reflection:	_____ _____ _____
10	Curve	When to Speak	Whoever interrupts the conversation of others to make a display of his fund of knowledge makes notorious his own stock of ignorance. Sa'id
		Comment:	When was the last time you interrupted somebody? What did you say? Was it worth the interruption? When was the last time someone interrupted you? How did you feel?
		Reflection:	_____ _____ _____
11	Center	Deafness	None so deaf as he that will not hear. Thomas Fuller
		Comment:	What do you refuse to hear?
		Reflection:	_____ _____ _____

Coming Out

Station	Direction	Symbol	Description/Reflection
11	Center	Life	Words form the thread on which we string our experiences. Aldous Huxley
		Comment:	What words describe your life? Your experiences? You?
		Reflection:	_____ _____ _____
12	Bend	Persuade	The passions are the only orators which always persuade. La Rochefoucauld
		Comment:	How do you express your passions? Are you passionate when you express yourself? How do you know? Is it effective?
		Reflection:	_____ _____ _____
13	Bend	Words	All words are pegs to hang ideas on. Henry Ward Beecher
		Comment:	What words do you use when you are sharing your ideas? Do others understand your words?
		Reflection:	_____ _____ _____
14	Curve	Style	A word is not the same with one writer as with another. Charles Peguy
		Comment:	Do you use quotations or phrases spoken by others? How can you make them your own?

		Reflection:	
15	Curve	Say Something	Writing comes more easily if you have something to say. Sholem Asch
		Comment:	What do you have to say? What do you want to say? Do you always say it? How?
		Reflection:	
16	Curve	Power	The pen is mightier than the sword. Bulwer-Lyiton
		Comment:	Think about a time when someone wrote something that hurt you. What did they write? Where did they write it? Who saw it? How did it make you feel?
		Reflection:	
17	Bend	Good Writing	In good writing, words become one with things. Ralph Waldo Emerson
		Comment:	Do you use the right words for the right reasons? Are they in order? Are they used grammatically correctly? Do you need to brush up on your grammar?
		Reflection:	
18	Curve	The Pen	The pen is a formidable weapon, but a man can kill himself with it a great deal more easily than he can other people. George Dennison Prentice

		Comment:	Have you ever written something to injure another and it came back to haunt you? What did you learn?
		Reflection:	_____ _____ _____
19	Bend	Adjectives	Pick adjectives as you would a diamond. Stanley Walker
		Comment:	When you describe something you allow others to draw pictures in their minds. Is their picture the same as your description?
		Reflection:	_____ _____ _____
20	Curve	Vocabulary	The man who uses big words is afraid that if people knew what he was talking about, they'd know he didn't know what he was talking about.
		Comment:	Is you language simple enough to be understood but sophisticated enough to show your learning?
		Reflection:	_____ _____ _____
21	Out	Say/Do	95% of American managers today say the right thing. 5% actually do it. James O'Toole
		Comment:	Do you do what you say you will?
		Reflection:	_____ _____ _____

Laberinto #14
Character Education

Going In

Station	Direction	Symbol	Description/Reflection
1	In	Conscience	The measure of a man's real capacity is what he would do if he felt he would never be found out. Lord Macaulay
		Comment:	Think about something you got away with? Would you do it again? Why or why not?
		Reflection:	_____ _____ _____
2	Curve	Honor	Honour has not to be won; it has only to be lost. Authur Schopenhauer
		Comment:	Are you an honorable person? Why or why not? Do you know someone who is? What is an honorable person?
		Reflection:	_____ _____ _____
3	Curve	Worthiness	It is not the oath that makes us believe the man, but the man the oath. Aeschylus
		Comment:	What are you sworn to do? Do you abide by your oath? Why or why not?
		Reflection:	_____ _____ _____
4	Curve	Truth	It is good to be truthful, but honesty should be exercised with care. Confucius

		Comment:	How can honesty be dangerous?
		Reflection:	_____ _____ _____
5	Curve	Flexibility	If anyone can demonstrate to me and convince me that I am thinking or acting incorrectly, I will happily change, for I wish to know the truth which never caused indignity to anyone. Marcus Aurelius
		Comment:	Have you ever admitted being wrong and changed your behavior, attitude or mind?
		Reflection:	_____ _____ _____
6	Curve	Calm	The growth of wisdom may be measured exactly by the diminution of ill temper. Friedrich W. Nietzche
		Comment:	Are you calm or do you have a hot temper easily aroused?
		Reflection:	_____ _____ _____
7	Bend	Independent	If man does not keep pace with his companions perhaps it is because he hears a different drummer. Let him step to the music which he hears however measured or far away. Henry David Thoreau
		Comment:	What music do you follow? Why do you follow it? Or why do you not?
		Reflection:	_____ _____ _____
8	Curve	Action	A tree is known by its fruit, a man by his deeds. St. Basil the Great

		Comment:	What are you known for? What will you be known for? Why?
		Reflection:	_____ _____ _____
9	Bend	Mentorship	We make a living by what we get, but we make a life by what we give. Winston Churchill
		Comment:	What do you give? Why?
		Reflection:	_____ _____ _____
10	Curve	Eloquence	A thing is not necessarily false because it is badly expressed, nor true because it is expressed magnificently. St. Augustine of Hippo
		Comment:	How do you rate your eloquence when speaking the truth? When speaking a falsehood?
		Reflection:	_____ _____ _____
11	Center	Secret of the World	Nobody, not even the poet, knows the secrets of the world. Federico Garcia Lorea
		Comment:	Because you are your own world and only you know its secrets. Think of three secrets you are keeping. Why do you keep them?
		Reflection:	_____ _____ _____

Coming Out

Station	Direction	Symbol	Description/Reflection
11	Center	Healthy	When health is absent, wisdom cannot reveal itself, art cannot manifest, strength cannot fight, wealth becomes useless and intelligence cannot be applied. Herophilus
		Comment:	Are you healthy? Why or why not?
		Reflection:	_____ _____ _____
12	Bend	Selective	One cannot weep for the entire world: it is beyond human strength. One must choose. Jean Anouilh
		Comment:	What do you choose to champion? Why?
		Reflection:	_____ _____ _____
13	Bend	Association	Tell me who your friends are and I will tell you who you are. Ancient Assyrian Proverb
		Comment:	Who do you associate with? Why? Who would you like to associate with? Why? What can you do to associate with them?
		Reflection:	_____ _____ _____
14	Curve	Teacher	The greatest good you can do for another is just not to share your riches but to reveal to him, his own. Benjamin Disraeli
		Comment:	Do you let others know their talents? Why or why not?

		Reflection:	_____ _____ _____
15	Curve	Purposeful	One of the greatest diseases is to be nobody to anybody. Mother Theresa
		Comment:	Are you somebody to somebody? Why or why not? Is somebody somebody to you? Why?
		Reflection:	_____ _____ _____
16	Curve	Self-Control	He who masters others has power. He who masters himself has strength. Laozi
		Comment:	What are your strengths? How can you improve them?
		Reflection:	_____ _____ _____
17	Bend	Self-Worth	He who undervalues himself is justly undervalued by others. William Hazlitt
		Comment:	How do you rate your self-worth? Why? How can you improve it?
		Reflection:	_____ _____ _____
18	Curve	Unspoken	As long as a word remains unspoken, you are its master; once you utter it, you are its slave. Ibn Gabirol
		Comment:	Do you think before you speak? Have your words ever gotten you into trouble? What did you do next? Why?
		Reflection:	_____ _____ _____

19	Bend	Courage	Whatever is to be your fate—face it. Abu Sa'id
		Comment:	What do you not want to face? Why? What is the worst that can happen? What is the best that can happen?
		Reflection:	
20	Curve	Time-Management	Take care of each moment and you take care of all time. The Buddha
		Comment:	How do you spend each moment? How many moments a day do you lose? Why?
		Reflection:	
21	Out	Grateful	Remember that what you have now was once among the things you only hoped for. Epicurus
		Comment:	How did you achieve what you have achieved? How can you continue to achieve what you want to achieve?
		Reflection:	

Laberinto #15
Quality

Going In

Station	Direction	Symbol	Description/Reflection
1	In	Good Enough	There will always be a conflict between "good" and "good enough." Henry M. Leland
		Comment:	Are your products/services good or good enough? Why?
		Reflection:	_____ _____ _____
2	Curve	Conse-quences	Revolutions often begin with the intention of only improving the systems they eventually bring down. The American, French and Russian revolutions all started as efforts to ameliorate the rule of a monarch, not to end it. Reform turns into revolt when the old system proves too rigid to adapt. So, too, the revolution that has destroyed the traditional corporation began with efforts to improve it. Michael Hammer
		Comment:	What revolution of quality is occurring in your company now? How are you involved? How did it begin? How will it end?
		Reflection:	_____ _____ _____
3	Curve	Bigger	Bigger isn't necessarily better; better is better. Patrick Townsend and Joan Gebhardt

		Comment:	What does your company do big? What does your company do right?
		Reflection:	
4	Curve	Rare	Excellent things are rare. Plato
		Comment:	What does your company produce that is rare? What does your company produce that is excellent?
		Reflection:	
5	Curve	Passion	Quality is about passion and pride. Peters and Nancy Austin
		Comment:	What does your company have pride and passion in? How is it shown?
		Reflection:	
6	Curve	Measurable	Quality is not an abstraction; it is a measurable and manageable business issue. John Guaspari
		Comment:	How does your company measure quality?
		Reflection:	
7	Bend	Journey	TQM is not a destination, but a journey toward improvement. V. Daniel Hunt
		Comment:	Does your company have a TQM system in place? Why or why not? Is it effective? Why or why not?
		Reflection:	

8	Curve	Standards	There can be no improvements where there are no standards. Masaaki Imai
		Comment:	What are your company's standards for quality? Are they too low or too high? Are they realistic? How are they communicated?
		Reflection:	_____ _____ _____
9	Bend	Culture	TQM does not and will not bring results overnight. The essence of TQM is a change of culture. Edward Sallis
		Comment:	Has your company's culture changed to embrace quality? Why or why not?
		Reflection:	_____ _____ _____
10	Curve	Effort	Quality improvement is a do-it-your-self effort. Steven George
		Comment:	Is your company doing it? By itself? Is it working? Why or why not?
		Reflection:	_____ _____ _____
11	Center	Excellence	We are what we repeatedly do. Excellence then, is not an act, but a habit. Aristotle
		Comment:	What are your company's habits? Are they effective?
		Reflection:	_____ _____ _____

Coming Out

Station	Direction	Symbol	Description/Reflection
11	Center	Commitment	Unless commitment is made there are only promises and hopes but no plans. Peter Drucker
		Comment:	Are you committed? Is your company committed?
		Reflection:	_____ _____ _____
12	Bend	Kaizen	The message of kaizen strategy is that not a day should go by without some kind of improvement being made somewhere in the company. Masaaki Imai
		Comment:	How do you make improvements every day? What gets improved every day in your company?
		Reflection:	_____ _____ _____
13	Bend	Right	Do it right the first time. Philip Crosby
		Comment:	Why are things done wrong in your company? How can you eliminate that?
		Reflection:	_____ _____ _____
14	Curve	Team	Just putting a bunch of people in a room together does not a team make. Howard Gitlow and Shelly Gitlow
		Comment:	Does your company have effective teams? Why or why not? What can you do to make them more effective? What can you do to be a better team member?

		Reflection:	_____ _____ _____
15	Curve	Maintenance	Quality needs to be constantly improved, but it is just as necessary to make sure that quality never deteriorates. Shigeru Mizunok
		Comment:	How do you maintain quality at your company?
		Reflection:	_____ _____ _____
16	Curve	Thorough	Be thorough, take nothing for granted. Katsuyoshi Ishihara
		Comment:	What details does your company overlook? How can this backfire?
		Reflection:	_____ _____ _____
17	Bend	Necessity	When necessity speaks, it demands. Russian Proverb
		Comment:	Why? What necessity is demanding your attention right now?
		Reflection:	_____ _____ _____
18	Curve	Success	Success is simple. Do what's right, the right way, at the right time. Arnold Glasgow
		Comment:	Does your company do this? Do you?
		Reflection:	_____ _____ _____
19	Bend	Statistics	Statistics are no substitute for judgment. Henry Clay

		Comment:	What statistics does your company hide behind when it comes to quality of its products and/or services?
		Reflection:	_____ _____ _____
20	Curve	What Matters	It is quality rather than quantity that matters. Seneca
		Comment:	How do you rate quality vs. quantity in your company? How can you improve it?
		Reflection:	_____ _____ _____
21	Out	All the Way	If you aren't going all the way, why go at all? Joe Namath
		Comment:	Answer the question.
		Reflection:	_____ _____ _____

Laberinto #16
Passion

Going In

Station	Direction	Symbol	Description/Reflection
1	In	Moderation	If passion drives you let reason hold the reins. Benjamin Franklin
		Comment:	Have you ever let passion take over? How did reason gain back control? How did it make you feel?
		Reflection:	_____ _____ _____
2	Curve	Reward	The reward of a thing well done is to have done it. Ralph Waldo Emerson
		Comment:	Are you always satisfied when you finish a job or task if no one recognizes you for it? Why or why not?
		Reflection:	_____ _____ _____
3	Curve	Ability	Whenever you are asked if you can do a job tell 'em "certainly I can!" Then get busy and find out how to do it. Theodore Roosevelt
		Comment:	Think about a time you tried something you were not sure you could do and it turned out well. What did you learn?
		Reflection:	_____ _____ _____

4	Curve	Success	A strong passion for any object will ensure success for the desire of the end will point out the means. William Hazlitt
		Comment:	Have you ever done something you did not want to do in order to get what you wanted? Why? How did you feel?
		Reflection:	_____ _____ _____
5	Curve	Soul	Only passions, great passions, can elevate the soul to great things. Denis Diderot
		Comment:	What inspires you to do things?
		Reflection:	_____ _____ _____
6	Curve	Accomplish	Nothing great in the world has been accomplished without passion. Hegel
		Comment:	What inspires you to do great things?
		Reflection:	_____ _____ _____
7	Bend	Slavery	When the passions become masters, they are vices. Pascal
		Comment:	Can you control your passions? Do you know someone who can't?
		Reflection:	_____ _____ _____
8	Curve	Enthusiasm	Every great and commanding moment in the annals of the world is the triumph of some enthusiasm. Ralph Waldo Emerson

		Comment:	What cause do you champion? Why? Is there a champion for a cause you admire? Why?
		Reflection:	_____ _____ _____
9	Bend	Feed	All the passions seek whatever nourishes them; fear loves the idea of danger. Joseph Joubert
		Comment:	What feeds your passion?
		Reflection:	_____ _____ _____
10	Curve	Half-Heart-edness	Half-heartedness never won a battle. William McKinley
		Comment:	Do you put everything you have into the task at hand? Why or why not?
		Reflection:	_____ _____ _____
11	Center	Desire	All human activity is prompted by desire. Bertrand Russell
		Comment:	What do you desire? Why? Can you obtain it? Achieve it? Why or why not?
		Reflection:	_____ _____ _____

Coming Out

Station	Direction	Symbol	Description/Reflection
11	Center	Bliss	Follow your bliss. Joseph Campbell
		Comment:	What is your bliss? Are you following it? Why or why not?
		Reflection:	_____ _____ _____
12	Bend	Difficulty	Difficulty is the excuse history never accepts. Edward R. Murrow
		Comment:	What excuses do you give when you cannot accomplish something? Why?
		Reflection:	_____ _____ _____
13	Bend	Too Much	Who begins too much accomplishes little. German Proverb
		Comment:	Do you have too much on your plate? Do you have too much unfinished? How can you streamline?
		Reflection:	_____ _____ _____
14	Curve	Deception	The easiest person to deceive is oneself. Edward Bulwer-Lutton
		Comment:	What are you lying to yourself about? Why? What is the truth? Why can't you accept it?
		Reflection:	_____ _____ _____
15	Curve	To Get Ahead	The passion to get ahead is sometimes born of the fear lest we be left behind. Eric Hoffer

		Comment:	What are you afraid of being left behind of? Why?
		Reflection:	_____ _____ _____
16	Curve	Belief	I am always at a loss to know how much to believe of my own stories. Washington Irving
		Comment:	Are you too caught up in your own stories that you can't tell what is real and what is not?
		Reflection:	_____ _____ _____
17	Bend	Zeal	Zeal without knowledge is fire without light. Thomas Fuller
		Comment:	Do you know enough about what you are passionate about?
		Reflection:	_____ _____ _____
18	Curve	Excitement	It you don't generate excitement, you don't generate much. Bill Marriott
		Comment:	What do you generate excitement about? What excites you? Why?
		Reflection:	_____ _____ _____
19	Bend	Astound	If we all did the things we are capable of doing we would literally astound ourselves. Thomas Edison
		Comment:	What are you capable of doing? Achieving? Why haven't you done it? Will you do it now? Why or why not?

		Reflection:	_____ _____ _____
20	Curve	Energy	The world belongs to the energetic. Ralph Waldo Emerson
		Comment:	How much energy do you have? How can you get more? How can you use it effectively?
		Reflection:	_____ _____ _____
21	Out	Do it Big	Do it big or stay in bed. Larry Kelly
		Comment:	Why do you get up in the morning?
		Reflection:	_____ _____ _____

Laberinto #17
Bonus Business Wisdom (3)

Going In

Station	Direction	Symbol	Description/Reflection
1	In	Problems	Problems are only opportunities in work clothes. Henry K. Raiser
		Comment:	What problems are you avoiding? Why?
		Reflection:	_____ _____ _____
2	Curve	Trivial	The most important events are often determined by very trivial causes. Cicero
		Comment:	What little things have happened to you or your company lately? How might they turn big?
		Reflection:	_____ _____ _____
3	Curve	Success	I failed my way to success. Thomas Edison
		Comment:	What have you failed at? What did you learn by failing?
		Reflection:	_____ _____ _____
4	Curve	Six Honest Men	I keep six honest men (they taught me all I knew), their names are What and Why and When and how and Where and Who. Rudyard Kipling
		Comment:	What questions do you ask? Why?

		Reflection:	
5	Curve	Counting	Not everything that counts can be counted; not everything that can be counted counts. Albert Einstein
		Comment:	What do you count? Is it countable? Does it count? What are you not counting? Why?
		Reflection:	
6	Curve	Preparation	The meeting of preparation and opportunity generates the offspring we call luck. Anthony Robbins
		Comment:	Using that definition, how can you be more lucky?
		Reflection:	
7	Bend	Responsibility	I believe that every right implies a responsibility; every opportunity an obligation; every possession, a duty. John D. Rockefeller
		Comment:	What are your responsibilities, your obligations, your duties?
		Reflection:	
8	Curve	Giants	If I have seen further, it is by standing on the shoulders of giants. Isaac Newton
		Comment:	Who should you be grateful to for your current position? Whose shoulders do you stand on?

		Reflection:	
9	Bend	Necessary	Make yourself necessary to some-one. Ralph Waldo Emerson
		Comment:	Are you necessary? To whom? Why?
		Reflection:	
10	Curve	Sources	He is wise who knows the sources of knowledge, who knows who has written, and where it is to be found. AA Hodge
		Comment:	Do you know where to go if you need to know something? Who? Where?
		Reflection:	
11	Center	For Others	It is more easy to be wise for others than for ourselves. La Rochefou-cauld
		Comment:	Why?
		Reflection:	

Coming Out

Station	Direction	Symbol	Description/Reflection
11	Center	Heart	At the heart of your being lies your answer. You know who you are and what you want. Laozi
		Comment:	Who are you? What do you want?
		Reflection:	_____ _____ _____
12	Bend	Loneli-ness	The worst loneliness is not to be comfortable with yourself. Mark Twain
		Comment:	Are you comfortable with yourself? Why or why not? What can you do about it?
		Reflection:	_____ _____ _____
13	Bend	Happiness	Happiness is mostly a by-product of doing what makes us feel fulfilled. Dr. Benjamin Spock
		Comment:	What makes you feel fulfilled? Are you doing it? How often? Can you do it more often? Why or why not?
		Reflection:	_____ _____ _____
14	Curve	Everything	He who wants to do everything will never do anything. Andre Maurios
		Comment:	Are you doing too much? What can you cut out?
		Reflection:	_____ _____ _____

15	Curve	Best	The best place to succeed is where you are with what you have. Charles M. Schwab
		Comment:	Look around you. What can you use to move ahead?
		Reflection:	_____ _____ _____
16	Curve	Look in the Eye	Never bend your head. Always hold it high. Look the world straight in the eye. Helen Keller
		Comment:	Do you look the world straight in the eye? Why or why not?
		Reflection:	_____ _____ _____
17	Bend	Standards	The quality of a leader is reflected in the standards they set for themselves. Ray Kroc
		Comment:	What are your standards for yourself? Where did you get them from? Do they work for you? Are you reaching them? Why or why not?
		Reflection:	_____ _____ _____
18	Curve	Correct	The right man is the one who seizes the moment. Johann Wolfgang von Goethe
		Comment:	Are you seizing the moment? Have you ever? How did it feel? Can you do it again?
		Reflection:	_____ _____ _____
19	Bend	Think	Wealth is the product of man's capacity to think. Ayn Rand

		Comment:	Are you thinking of ways to become more wealthy? What does wealth mean to you?
		Reflection:	
20	Curve	Influence	The key to successful leadership is influence, not authority. Kenneth Blanchard
		Comment:	Who do you influence? Why? Who do you want to influence to be successful? How can you make it happen?
		Reflection:	
21	Out	Doubts	The only limit to our realization of tomorrow will be our doubts of today. Franklin D Roosevelt
		Comment:	What doubts do you have about your own abilities? Why? How can you get rid of your doubts?
		Reflection:	

Appendices

Laberinto Template In

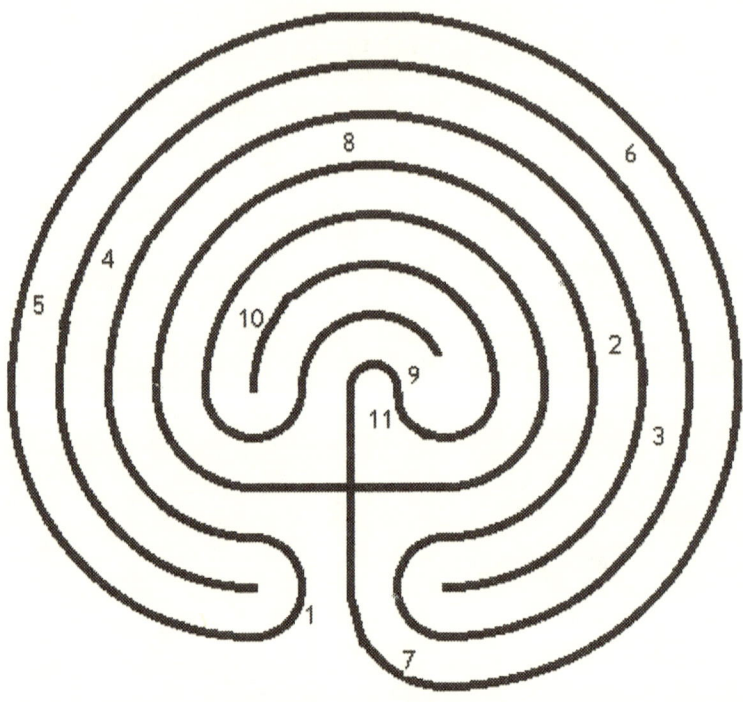

Figure 1: Going In (1–11)

Laberinto Template Out

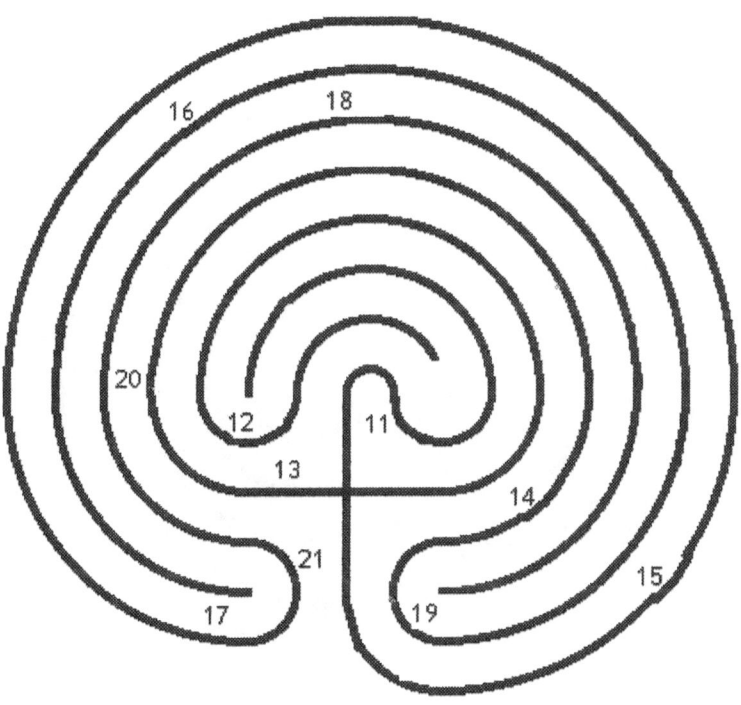

Figure 2: Coming Out (11–21)

Laberinto Template In/Out

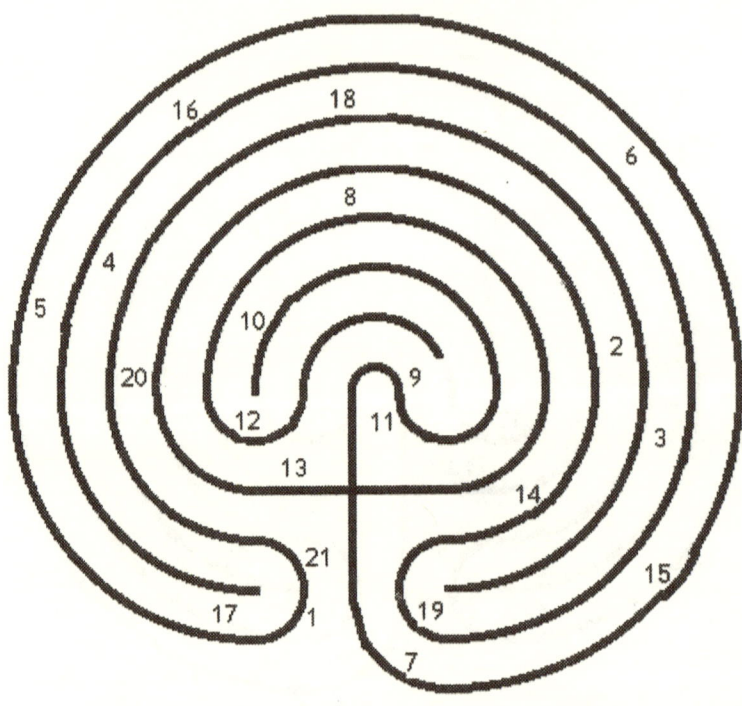

Figure 3: Going In & Coming Out (1–21)

References—Books

Baker, Daniel B., <u>PowerQuotes</u>, Detroit: Visible Ink Press, 1992, ISBN: 1-57859-014-0

Bartlett, John, <u>Bartlett's Familiar Quotations, 16th Edition</u>, Boston: Little, Brown and Company, 1992, ISBN: 0-316-08277-5

Berg, Christopher, <u>Amazing Art: Wonders of the Ancient World</u>, NY: HarperCollin, 2001, ISBN: 0-06-095674-7

Camp, Wesley D., <u>Camp's Unfamiliar Quotations from 2000 BC to the Present</u>, NJ: Prentice Hall, 1990, ISBN: 0-13-619081-2

Candolini, Gernot, <u>Labyrinths: Walking Toward the Center</u>, NY: The Crossroad Publishing Company, 2003, ISBN: 0-8245-2102-1

Cook, John, <u>The Book of Positive Quotations</u>, MI: Fairview Press, 1996, ISBN: 1-57749-053-3

Curry, Helen, <u>TheWay of the Labyrinth: A Powerful Mediation for Everyday Life</u>, NY: Penguin Compass, 2000, ISBN: 0-14-019617-X

Edwards, Tryon, <u>The New Dictionary of Thoughts</u>, Standard Book Company, 1959

Ehrlich, Eugene and Marshall de Bruhl, <u>The International Thesaurus of Quotations</u>, NY: Harper Collins, 1996, ISBN: 0-06-273373-7

Ehrlich, Henry, The Wiley Book of Business Quotations, NY: John Wiley & Sons, 1998, ISBN: 0-471-18207-9

Esar, Evan, 20,000 Quips & Quotes, NY: Barnes & Noble, 1995, ISBN: 1-56619-529-2

Fisher, Adrian and Georg Gerster, The Art of the Maze, NY: Sterling Publishing, 2000, ISBN: 1-84188-025-6

Fisher, Adrian and Howard Loxton, Secrets of the Maze: An Interactive Guide to the World's Most Amazing Mazes, NY: Barron's Educational Services, 1997, ISBN: 0-7641-5053-7

Gomes, Helio, Quality Quotes, WI: ASQC Quality Press, 1996, ISBN: 0-87389-407-3

Kern, Hermann, Through the Labyrinth: Designs and Meanings over 5,000 Years, NY:Prestel, 2000, ISBN: 3-79132-144-7

McWilliams, Peter, The Life 101 Quote Book, CA: Prelude Press Inc., 1996, ISBN: 0-931580-68-4

Murphy, Edward F., 2,715 One-Line Quotations for Speakers, Writers & Reaconteurs, NY: Gramercy Books, 1996, ISBN: 0-517-68236-2

Ross, David, 1001 Pearls of Wisdom, London: Duncan Barid Publishers, Ltd., 2006, ISBN: 0-7394-6128-1

Saward, Jeff, Labyrinths & Mazes: A Complete Guide to Magical Paths of the World, NY: Lark Books, 2003, ISBN: 1-57990-539-0

Seldes, George, The Great Thoughts, NY: Ballantine Books, 1985, ISBN: 0-345-29887-X

Westbury, Virginia, Labyrinths: Ancient Paths of Wisdom and Peace, Da Capo Press, 2001, ISBN: 0-306-81310-6

References—Web Sites

Quotations Page
http://www.quotationspage.com

Quote Doctor
http://www.quotedoctor.com

About.Com Quotations
http://quotations.about.com

Technology Quotes
http://whatis.techtarget.com

Deborah Gonzalez, Esq.

Deborah Gonzalez, Esq. is Executive Vice-President of Parker Associates International (PAI), an international consulting company based in Wayne, New Jersey, that has been offering management training and consulting and economic development services to firms and government organizations in the United States, as well as Eastern and Western Europe, Africa and South America for over forty years.

Deborah is a renaissance executive with an eclectic educational background that combines business, legal, and technology skills with hands-on experience. This includes twenty + years of experience in corporate business consulting and training; including international projects in Eastern and Western Europe focusing on marketing, quality management, and technology transfer. This combination of knowledge and experience has lead to the cultivation of the skills of interconnecting and interrelating disparate trends and assets in a network of resources and global contacts.

In addition, Deborah is a licensed New York attorney focusing on intellectual property asset protection and management, including international licensing, Internet and cyber law regulation and international transaction contracts. She is a member of the New York Bar Association, the American Bar Association, and the New Jersey Association of Professional Mediators.

Deborah has designed and created unique training and curriculum for business professionals as well as international diplomats—including economic and community development programmes for corporations and higher education institutions; for example a MAS program for United Nations diplomats in Diplomacy and International Relations for a Northern New Jersey University, which includes specific partnerships with country governments, public institutions and colleges abroad.

Deborah is known for her ability to integrate history into her business projects, finding new and innovative ways to explore how ancient tools can help her modern day clients achieve the success they are seeking. *Laberinto* is a continuation of her research and work in this anthropological endeavor.

Subscribe to
The Laberinto Newsletter

Enjoyed the laberintos presented in the book but want more?

A one-year, 6-issue subscription to
The Laberinto Newsletter
is just the solution you've been seeking!

Every other month you will receive by e-mail or hard-copy a newsletter containing 2 new business laberintos and interesting articles full of advice and tips on achieving and enhancing your business success.

Just fill out the form below and mail with a check made out to *Deborah Gonzalez;* Parker Associates International, 91 Myrtle Avenue, Edgewater, NJ 07020. Make sure you indicate if you want it electronically or by regular mail. Overseas subscriptions should add $60 to the hard copy fee for regular mail.

[   ] Yes, I would like to order a subscription to The Laberinto Newsletter. I understand I will receive 6 issues a year (one every other month) in the format I have selected below. I am including my payment by check and look forward to my first issue.

[   ] $35, Electronic; e-mail address for digital delivery: _____
[   ] $60, Hard copy; address for delivery below.
[   ] $120, Hard copy; International; address for delivery below.

Want a customized
Business Laberinto
For your company, organization
or business?

Then contact *Deborah Gonzalez, Esq.* at
laberinto@att.net

Also available for corporate trainings, workshops and conferences.

978-0-595-40730-9
0-595-40730-7

www.ingramcontent.com/pod-product-compliance
Lightning Source LLC
Chambersburg PA
CBHW031049180526
45163CB00002BA/759